modern maple

Minnesota Historical
Society Press

modern maple

teresa marrone

the Northern plate

the ⸰ orthern plate

Modern Maple is the second book in the Northern Plate series, celebrating the bounty of the Upper Midwest by focusing on a single ingredient, exploring its historical uses as well as culinary applications across a range of dishes. *Rhubarb Renaissance* by Kim Ode is the first book in the series.

Text and recipes ©2013 by Teresa Marrone. Design © Minnesota Historical Society. All rights reserved. No part of this book may be used or reproduced in any manner whatsoever without written permission except in the case of brief quotations embodied in critical articles and reviews. For information, write to the Minnesota Historical Society Press, 345 Kellogg Blvd. W., St. Paul, MN 55102–1906.

www.mhspress.org

The Minnesota Historical Society Press is a member of the Association of American University Presses.

Manufactured in the United States of America

10 9 8 7 6 5 4 3 2 1

♾ The paper used in this publication meets the minimum requirements of the American National Standard for Information Sciences—Permanence for Printed Library Materials, ANSI Z39.48–1984.

International Standard Book Number
ISBN: 978-0-87351-888-8 (paper)

LIBRARY OF CONGRESS CATALOGING-IN-PUBLICATION DATA
Marrone, Teresa.
Modern maple / Teresa Marrone.
    pages cm. — (The northern plate)
Includes bibliographical references and index.
ISBN 978-0-87351-888-8 (pbk. : alk. paper)
1. Sugar maple—Tapping. 2. Maple syrup. I. Title.

SB239.M3M37 2013
641.6'364—dc23

2012040513

....

Modern Maple was designed and set in type by Cathy Spengler.
The typefaces are Chaparral, TheSans, and Questal.

In loving memory of our beautiful parrot, Tuca, who was the light in our household.

Special thanks to Deb and Oscar Meyer, for assistance in developing, testing, and tasting quite a few of these recipes; to Mary Althaus, who supplied me with numerous photo props and also helped in the tasting department (and carried quite a few plates of calories out of my house); and to my husband, Bruce Bohnenstingl, who is always willing to try anything I put on the table.

contents

introduction

a maple tree is a lovely thing. Its hard, fine-grained wood is used to craft beautiful furniture and specialty items as diverse as bowling pins, butcher blocks, and stringed instruments. In summer, its lush canopy of leaves provides welcome shade, and in fall, those same leaves—minus their chlorophyll, which provides the green hue—adorn cityscapes, fencerows, and lakeshores with their stunning displays of autumn color. Some would argue, however, that late winter to early spring is the maple's finest time, for that is when groundwater pumping through the wood of the tree, rising from the roots to the branch tips, can be tapped to make maple syrup.

FROM TREE TO TABLE

Like all trees, maples draw groundwater through *sapwood,* the living, woody tissue just under the bark, sending the sap up to the branches to nourish buds, leaves, and fruits (those flat, wing-shaped "helicopters" are the fruits). As the water travels through the sapwood, it picks up stored nutrients—most importantly for syrup-makers, sucrose. In late winter, maples begin to awaken from dormancy, and when air temperatures rise above freezing the roots begin drawing water to send to the branches above. When temperatures fall below freezing at night, the trees stop drawing water, but the next time the temperatures rise above freezing, the roots begin drawing again. Sap is collected during the time this freeze-thaw cycle occurs regularly—often a period of just a few weeks. When temperatures stay above freezing overnight and the buds at branch tips begin to develop, the sap flows continuously; at this point it picks up too many impurities from the wood and becomes dark and cloudy—referred to as *buddy*—and is no longer suitable for syrup-making.

When it comes from the tree, maple sap looks just like water. It has a slightly sweet taste; sugar maple sap typically contains about 2 percent sugar. It must be boiled or otherwise reduced so that the sugar concentration is 66 percent. The rule of thumb is that it takes forty gallons of sap to produce one gallon of finished syrup (think about *that* next time you're drenching your pancakes!). For centuries, maple syrup has been produced by boiling to reduce the water content (although freezing has also been used to concentrate the sugar: see page 7). In the 1980s, numerous maple producers started using reverse osmosis equipment to eliminate much of the water; the remaining sap requires a far shorter cooking time to achieve the proper sugar concentration, saving both time and fuel.

All maple trees that are native to our area can be tapped for syrup-making. The sugar maple is considered the best due to the quality of its sap, which generally has a higher sugar content than sap from other maples. Sugar maples are abundant in most of the Upper Midwest, both in the wild and in cultivation, and are known for their hot-poker-red fall display. Four other native maples are also used for syrup-making, especially by hobbyists who don't mind their lower yields. Silver maple is abundant in the wild and also commonly used in landscaping due to its rapid growth. Red maple and black maple are less common in the wild in our area, but both are planted as ornamentals; black maple is often tapped by commercial operations in the states south of the Great Lakes, where it grows more commonly, because its sap has a sugar content close to that of sugar maple. Boxelder sap can also be used to make maple syrup. While its leaves don't resemble the iconic maple leaf displayed proudly on the Canadian flag, the boxelder is, indeed, a maple, although the sugar content of its sap is lower than any other maple used for syrup-making. The Norway maple is an introduced (nonnative) species commonly used in landscaping; its sap is cloudy and not suitable for syrup-making.[1]

Other than boxelder, none of these maples grow in the western half of the United States. Some grow in the Southeast, but the southern climate doesn't produce the extended daily freeze-thaw cycles required for adequate sap production. *All* commercially produced maple syrup comes from the northeastern quarter of the United States and adjoining Canadian provinces, which have the unique combination of the proper types of trees and the extended freeze-thaw cycle needed to obtain enough sap for commercial processing. Quebec is the maple syrup leader, with 7.7 million gallons produced commercially in 2011; in that same year, commercial producers in the United States made 2.8 million gallons, of which 1.1 million came from Vermont and just under a half million from the Upper Midwest.[2]

Sap collected later in the season has a lower sugar content and so must be cooked longer, resulting in a darker finished product. Syrup is categorized or "graded" based on its color; the grading terms vary between the United States and Canada. The lightest syrup, which comes from the first sap of the season, is called Grade A Light Amber, Light Amber, or sometimes "fancy" in the United States; in Canada it is called No. 1 Extra Light. The next darker syrup is called Grade A Medium Amber or Medium Amber (No. 1 Light Grade A in Canada). Next is Grade A Dark Amber or Dark Amber (No. 1 Medium Grade A in Canada). Most syrup sold in supermarkets falls into one of these three classes.

In years past, what is referred to as Grade B syrup (No. 2 Amber in Canada) was rarely available to the consumer. This dark brown syrup, which is produced toward the end of the season, was used almost exclusively by commercial food producers; its stronger maple flavor was deemed inappropriate for home use (and, indeed, it would overwhelm pancakes if used straight out of the bottle). Savvy cooks, however, searched out sources of grade B to use in baked goods and other dishes where the strong maple flavor is a benefit. Increased demand has made grade B more readily available. I buy it at Trader Joe's, but there are other sources. I recommend it in some recipes in this book; although you may always use one of the more common grade A syrups in these recipes, the maple flavor will be much more pronounced if you use grade B. ◇

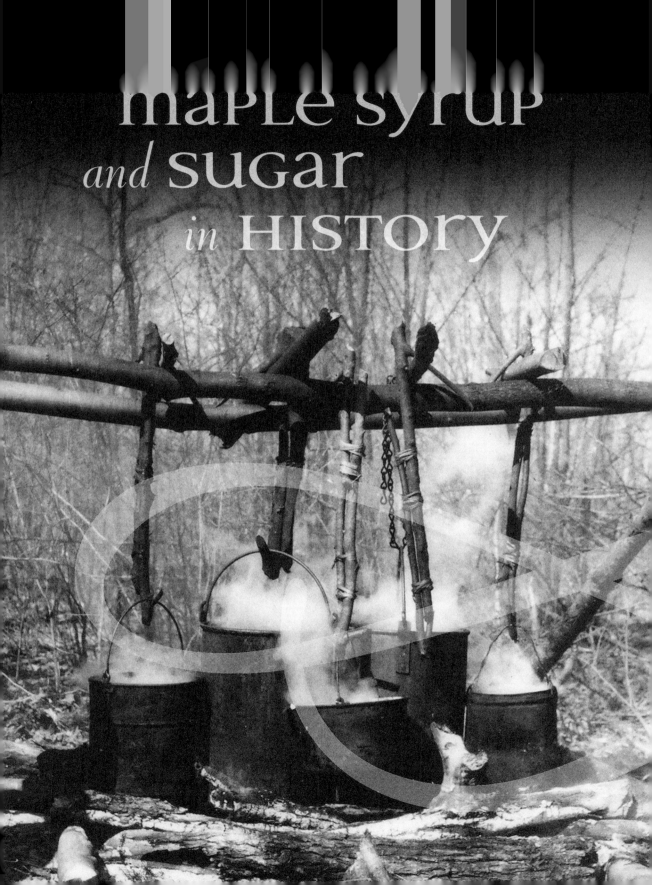

maple syrup
and sugar
in HISTORY

THE EARLY DAYS

Long before Europeans' arrival, American Indians in the Northeastern Woodlands—an area encompassing present-day New England, the mid-Atlantic states, the northern Ohio River Valley, and the states and provinces around the Great Lakes—used maple sap, syrup, and sugar in a variety of ways (as they continue to do today). In the seventeenth century, missionaries and explorers reported that Indians used fresh sap as a restorative drink and also employed it in food preparation.[3]

In addition to using the sap in its natural state, Indians harnessed both fire and ice to reduce the watery sap to its sweet essence, producing syrup and crystallized sugar. In the earliest days, Indians collected and processed sap in vessels made of birch bark or wood; red-hot stones were dropped into the vessels to boil off excess water, thereby concen-

Mrs. John Mink collecting maple sap, Mille Lacs, 1925 >

trating the sugar content of the remaining liquid to produce syrup. As an alternative, sap was poured into shallow vessels and allowed to freeze partially; the Indians repeatedly discarded the ice that formed on the surface, leaving behind ever-sweeter liquid that eventually was reduced to a sweet, thick, brown syrup. Increased contact with European fur traders in the 1700s provided Indians with heavy metal kettles which could be hung over a fire to make sap reduction far more efficient.[4]

Once the excess water had been boiled or frozen away, the resulting syrup could be further heated and then stirred until it crystallized to produce maple sugar, which was easier to store and transport than liquid syrup. Frances Densmore, an ethnographer who spent time with Ojibwe Indians (also called the Chippewa or, in their own language, *Anishinaabe*) on several Minnesota reservations at the start of the twentieth century, wrote a thorough description of making maple sugar in a paper published in 1928. She described "sugaring off," a process during which maple syrup was heated until thick, then "quickly transferred to the [wooden] granulating trough, where it was again stirred with a [maple-wood] paddle, and at the proper time 'rubbed or worked' with the back of the granulating ladle . . . This had to be done very rapidly before the sugar cooled too much . . . From the granulating trough the warm sugar was poured into *makuks*" (containers made of birch bark). Candies were also made by pouring the hot, thick syrup—before it was worked into crystalline granules—into small birch-bark or wooden containers, where it hardened; sometimes, the upper bill from a duck was used as a container, and once the syrup hardened, several were strung together as a treat for children.[5]

Maple sugar was a predominant seasoning for Eastern Woodland Indians and was apparently favored over salt among most tribes; indeed, many tribes had no access to salt and did not learn to use it until introduced to it by white traders and settlers. Densmore wrote, "A Canadian Chippewa said that in old times his people had no salt and

Mary Day
making maple
sugar, Mille Lacs,
1948 >

that more maple sugar was used as a seasoning than the quantity of
salt now used by white people. In the early days the Minnesota Chippewa had no salt and some of the older Indians have not yet acquired
a taste for it."[6]

Along with wild berries and animal fat, maple sugar was used by
Indians to season many foods, including wild rice dishes, soups, fish,
stews, and porridges; it was also mixed with cold water to make a re-
freshing beverage. The sugar was also of great economic importance to
eighteenth-century Indians, who traded it—along with furs and wild
rice—in exchange for European goods including firearms, tobacco, liquor, and metal items such as cookware.[7]

Colonists learned the art of sugaring from the Indians and used
emerging European technology to add their own improvements. Instead of slashing the bark of the trees as the Indians did in the early
days, colonists made hollow tubes called *spiles,* which were inserted

into holes they drilled in the trees using hand augers. The sap was collected in buckets—wooden at first, later metal—rather than birch-bark containers. The heavy buckets were carried on shoulder yokes (and, later, by horse) to metal boiling kettles. The colonists also used finely textured cloth to strain ash and other impurities from the syrup. The finished syrup and sugar were good alternatives to the cane sugar that was produced by slaves in the West Indies and which was subject to high tariffs at the time.

Thomas Jefferson attempted to start an American maple sugar industry in the late eighteenth century. Although his planting of sugar maples at Monticello failed to thrive, he promoted widespread cultivation of the sugar maple, writing in a 1791 letter to William Drayton (a budding politician who later became a congressman), "The attention now paying to the sugar-Maple tree promises us an abundant supply of sugar at home; and I confess I look with infinite gratification to the addition to the products of the U.S. of three such articles as oil, sugar, and upland rice."[8]

Quakers, fervent opponents of slavery since the late seventeenth century, were quick to seize upon the idea of American-produced maple sugar as an alternative to slave-produced West Indian sugar. Other Abolitionists soon joined in the clamor, which intensified in the years preceding the Civil War. In 1840, the March entry in the Vermont *Farmer's Almanac* urged, "All who have suitable trees should now be in readiness for the manufacture of maple sugar. He who now makes one pound of sugar from the produce of his own lands, adds so much to the stock of our national wealth; whereas that stock is diminished in the same degree by every pound purchased from abroad. Besides, sugar made at home must possess a sweeter flavor to an independent American of the north, than that which is mingled with the groans and tears of slavery." Although maple producers attempted to capture the sugar market in the United States, they could not compete with cane sugar from the West Indies, which by now was relatively cheap and readily available; nor could they take the maple flavor out of their sugar, which was brown rather than the pristine white of highly refined cane sugar.[9]

Eventually, however, maple products were accepted as specialty foods coveted for their unique flavor. Soon enough, food companies were producing "maple syrup" that was adulterated with cheap sugars including sorghum and corn products; some was made simply by boiling brown sugar in water. Mapleine, an imitation maple flavoring, was introduced by the Crescent Manufacturing Company at the Puyallup Fair in 1908 and soon was available on grocery store shelves. Pure maple syrup was still being produced, but the cost and availability relegated it to specialty status with most Americans.

World War II brought maple, and other American-made sugars, back to the forefront. Processed sugar had to be rationed during the war, so cooks adapted recipes to use substitutes such as honey, molasses, corn syrup, and maple syrup. Marion White, in her 1945 cookbook *Sweets Without Sugar*, wrote, "The sugar provided by ration will be adequate for the morning coffee and the evening tea. The real shortage will be felt in the kitchen by the housewife whose family craves good desserts. So it is here that we must make substitution." Her book provides over two hundred recipes using alternative sweeteners for "the rich dessert that finishes dinner so satisfactorily, the cakes and cookies that make afternoon tea an occasion, and the pies that keep American men in good spirit." (A recipe I adapted from *Sweets Without Sugar*, Wartime Nut Wafers, appears on page 147 of this book.)[10]

MAPLE SYRUP IN MODERN TIMES

Today, with the growing focus on artisanal and local foods, maple syrup is enjoying another culinary renaissance. No longer is maple syrup confined to the breakfast table; *au courant* chefs use it in dishes featuring everything from apricots to zucchini. Exposure to Asian cuisines that utilize sweet flavors in combination with salty, sour, and hot has emboldened cooks to try maple in spicy dipping sauces, stir-fries, and other savory dishes (actually, my German grandmother may have been ahead of the curve when, in the 1960s, she prepared her version of "chop suey" with a panoply of ingredients including maple syrup). Maple's affinity with various foods has added an entire category of dishes to the American cook's lexicon: who among us has not at least encountered a recipe for—if not eaten—pork tenderloin sautéed with apples and mustard-maple pan sauce, maple-glazed roasted root vegetables, or maple-cured smoked bacon and salmon?

Maple syrup from small producers and American Indian tribes has acquired the same cachet given to artisan-produced cheese, salami, bread, and other foods. Serious maple aficionados quaff tiny cups of various small-batch maple syrups to pick up subtle flavor differences, much in the way wine tasters judge wine. Anise, smoke, kiwi, nutmeg, and black licorice are just a few of the flavors noted by samplers. The North American Maple Syrup Council holds an annual competition to award prizes to the best maple syrup in each class. Although our area produces a very small proportion of the total annual volume of maple syrup, numerous small producers in the Upper Midwest have captured top honors over the years in this international competition.

There is a growing movement that believes maple syrup is a product with its own *terroir*—unique characteristics associated with a food product's place of origin. University of Vermont professor Dr. Amy Trubek has undertaken specialized tastings of maple syrup to determine if factors such as soil type and microclimates provide syrup with unique, identifiable nuances. Perhaps some time in the future, maple syrup will reach a status similar to that used for French and Italian wine and cheese, with its own system of geographical distinctions similar to the AOC/DOC (*Appellation d'Origine Contrôlée/Denominazione di Origine Controllata*) labeling.[11] ◇

maple *in the* KITCHEN

Without a doubt, the most familiar role of maple syrup is to top a stack of pancakes or a plate of French toast. Maple's uses extend far beyond that, however. It works surprisingly well with numerous spices and herbs, including cumin, cardamom, gingerroot, chipotle chile pepper, black pepper, Szechuan pepper, marjoram, sage, rosemary, and thyme (parsley, maybe not so much). Mustard is a natural partner, as are cinnamon, nutmeg, vanilla, and powdered ginger. A little vinegar helps balance the sweetness (too much, however, drowns out the subtleties). Maple pairs beautifully with fruits, particularly autumn fruits such as apples and pears. Bananas, pineapple, mangoes, and blueberries also work well with maple, and don't forget about dried fruits including cranberries, figs, apples, and apricots. A shot of maple added to onions during sautéeing helps caramelize them to rich, golden sweetness. Pork of all cuts and rich, oily fish such as salmon are elevated to new heights when prepared with a bit of maple syrup, which also helps them brown to deliciousness. Maple's affinity with smoked meats, particularly bacon and ham, is legendary. And let's not forget about root vegetables roasted with maple to enhance browning, butter blended with maple to produce rich sauces and confections, nuts glazed with maple syrup—the list goes on. Here are some tips to help you get the most out of maple in your kitchen.

WORKING WITH MAPLE SYRUP

Maple syrup is sticky stuff, and it tends to cling to measuring cups and spoons. If your recipe uses oil in the same step as maple syrup, measure the oil first: when you add the syrup to the measuring cup or spoon, it will slide out cleanly. If there's no oil in the recipe, you could coat the cup or spoon with cooking spray. Another option is to measure the maple first, then measure any milk or other thin liquid needed, using it to wash out the cup or spoon; you can also swirl a sticky measuring spoon in liquid that's about to be added to a recipe.

When I pour maple syrup from a measuring cup into a mixing bowl or saucepan, I'll often lay two chopsticks across the bowl and set the measuring cup upside-down on top of them, allowing it to drip into the bowl for a few minutes. I also prop an empty bottle of maple syrup upside-down in a bowl or measuring cup and let it drain for a few minutes; it's surprising how much syrup clings to the inside of a bottle. (If you warm the bottle first, the syrup will slide out more easily.)

Occasionally, sugar crystals will develop in the bottom of a jar of maple syrup; this happens much more frequently with home-produced syrup, but I've also seen it in commercial stuff. The crystals are just like the rock candy you may have made in high-school chemistry class and are completely edible. Place the jar in a pan of very hot water for a few minutes (or microwave it on medium power for ten seconds or so, if the jar is microwave safe), then carefully stir the crystals with a table knife to break them up. Use them to top ice cream, or stir them into a batch of cookies; they're also really good used as a topper on the Maple-Caramel Overnight Rolls on page 24.

REDUCING MAPLE SYRUP

Often you'll need to boil some maple syrup to reduce the volume of liquid and intensify the flavor. Maple syrup is made by boiling sap to 7 degrees above boiling to concentrate the sugar. When you reduce syrup to boost the flavor, you're cooking it to an even higher temperature to further concentrate the sugar. Anytime maple syrup is cooked much beyond 219 degrees, however, its structure changes, and when it cools it can become grainy, form crystals, or set up solid and brittle, depending on how high the temperature got and what was done to it during cooking and cooling. When controlled, these various forms can be used to produce, for example, a silky sauce, chewy caramels, rock-candy crystals, or hard candy.

If you want reduced syrup but don't want crystals or graininess, you can add something to prevent the structural changes. Cream or butter both work for this purpose; they can be added at the start of reducing (as in the Chocolate-Striped Maple Caramel Corn, page 54) or after the syrup has been reduced (as in the Maple-Caramel Overnight Rolls, page 24). Corn syrup can also help prevent crystallization. Like white sugar, maple syrup contains sucrose, but the sugar in corn syrup is glucose. The molecular difference between the two forms of sugar helps prevent the maple from forming crystals.

You'll need a heavy-bottomed pot or saucepan to reduce maple syrup; thinner pans scorch too easily because the heat is unevenly distributed. Choose a pan that is much larger than the volume of syrup you'll be cooking: it foams up quite a bit, and you definitely do not want a boilover of this stuff—it makes a hideous mess (speaking from experience). I have a 1-gallon soup pot that is 8 inches across and about 5 inches deep; I use this for quantities over 1 cup. For smaller batches, I use a medium saucepan that is 6¼ inches across; for even smaller quantities I have a small saucepan that is 5½ inches across. You'll also need a candy thermometer or a quick-read thermometer that can handle temperatures up to 325 degrees. Before you begin, check its accuracy as described on page 16 in "Testing a Thermometer."

When you're reducing syrup, you must devote your full attention to the task at hand; this is not the time for kitchen multitasking because syrup can overcook or boil over in the thirty seconds it takes to wipe down the counter. If you'll be adding ingredients such as butter or cream after the syrup reaches a certain temperature, have the ingredients measured and ready to hand *before* you start boiling the syrup. If the syrup threatens to boil over, remove it from the heat immediately, swirl the pan a bit to stop the bubbling, then reduce the heat before continuing. Keep your stove and work area neat and free of distracting clutter, and pay attention to what you're doing. Boiling syrup is way hotter than boiling water, and it sticks to your skin; a hasty movement that tips a saucepan could result in a very serious burn, so stay calm and be careful.

One of the biggest challenges in reducing a small volume of syrup is getting an accurate temperature reading. Most cooking thermometers are designed to be immersed an inch or more into the liquid being heated, but you'll rarely be cooking that volume of maple syrup; for example, a cup of syrup fills my small saucepan to a depth of less than one-half inch. Furthermore, the thermometer must be high enough that the tip isn't touching the bottom of the pan because the hot metal would provide an inaccurate reading.

It's helpful to tilt the pan to pool the syrup at one corner when you want to check the temperature; that way you'll have a deeper spot to immerse the tip of your thermometer. If you're using a quick-read thermometer rather than a clip-on candy thermometer, remember that even though these are often called "instant-read" they are far from it. You need to hold the tip in the boiling syrup until the temperature readout stabilizes, which could take a minute or longer. Use a nylon-tipped set of tongs to hold the thermometer with its tip in the syrup, and wear an oven mitt to protect your hand from the steam and heat.

TESTING A THERMOMETER

In this book, all recipes that call for cooking syrup to a certain temperature provide the "degrees above boiling" number as well as the standard number. The temperature of boiling water at sea level is 212 degrees, but individual thermometers may read a slightly different number; furthermore, the actual boiling temperature of water may be different at your exact location and may also change from day to day due to atmospheric conditions. Although it's extra work, it is really important to check the accuracy of your thermometer *each time* you use it for reducing syrup to a specific temperature. Candymakers are accustomed to taking this step when working with regular sugar, and the method is the same for maple.

Simply take the temperature of a pan of vigorously boiling water with the thermometer you'll be using, ensuring that you give the thermometer enough time to stabilize. Jot down the temperature of the boiling water, then add the "degrees above boiling" to that number and use the result as your target when following the recipe. For example, if your thermometer measures boiling water at 210 degrees and the recipe says to cook the syrup to 18 degrees above boiling, you should cook the syrup to a temperature of 228 degrees. This simple step ensures success—and you won't have to scrape a hardened mess out of your pan because you overcooked the syrup. When you're done cooking, remember that sticky spoons and pots with cooked-on maple usually clean up easily after a short soak in cold water. ✧

breakfast

Breakfast is the meal most folks associate with maple syrup, usually in its time-honored role as a topper for pancakes, waffles, and the like. It's much more than a one-trick pony, though, as you'll see in this chapter showcasing maple in other top-of-the-morning dishes such as smoothies, sweet sausage gravy, luscious caramel rolls, candied bacon, and a surprisingly delicious version of eggs Benedict with a maple-kissed hollandaise sauce.

Breakfast Bread Pudding with Praline Topping

Tender, custardy bread pudding gets topped with a sweet, crunchy praline mixture in this make-ahead breakfast dish. Serve it with fresh fruit salad.

SERVES 6

....

- 1 teaspoon unsalted butter, softened
- 1 loaf challah or other rich egg bread, unsliced (you won't use all of it)
- 5 large eggs
- 1½ cups whole milk
- 3 tablespoons maple syrup
- 1 teaspoon vanilla extract
- ⅛ teaspoon salt

PRALINE TOPPING

- 6 tablespoons (¾ stick) unsalted butter, very soft
- ½ cup packed light brown sugar
- ½ cup chopped pecans (about 2 ounces)
- 2 tablespoons maple syrup
- ½ teaspoon cinnamon

....

>>

Rub the teaspoon of butter evenly inside an 11x7–inch baking dish or casserole. Cut bread into 1-inch cubes, adding to the dish as you go. Continue until the dish is about three-quarters full, about 6 cups of cubes (10 to 12 ounces). In mixing bowl, beat eggs with a whisk until well mixed but not foamy. Add milk, 3 tablespoons syrup, vanilla, and salt; beat until well mixed. Pour over bread, stirring gently to coat all pieces. Cover dish with foil and refrigerate for at least 4 hours or as long as overnight.

When you're ready to bake, heat oven to 375 degrees. Remove dish from refrigerator and let it stand at room temperature while you make the praline topping. In a mixing bowl, stir butter vigorously with a spoon until smooth. Add brown sugar and stir to combine. Stir in the pecans, 2 tablespoons syrup, and cinnamon. Spoon small dollops on top of soaked bread, then spread out gently with the back of the spoon to cover the bread. Bake for 5 minutes, then reduce heat to 350 degrees and continue baking until mixture is set and golden brown, 40 to 45 minutes total. Serve warm, with additional maple syrup if you like. ◇

English Muffin and Berry "Hash"

Chunks of crisp French toast tossed with berries and maple syrup—what's not to love? SERVES 3–4

    2 eggs
    ½ cup milk
    ½ teaspoon vanilla extract
    ¼ teaspoon cinnamon
    pinch nutmeg
    pinch salt
    3 English muffins, split
    2 tablespoons unsalted butter
    ¼ cup maple syrup
    1 cup blueberries
    1 cup raspberries

In large mixing bowl, whisk together eggs, milk, vanilla, cinnamon, nutmeg, and salt. Cut split English muffins into ¾-inch squares, adding to egg mixture as you cut. When all English muffins have been cut and added, stir to coat. Set aside for 3 minutes, stirring once.

Melt butter in large skillet over medium heat. When butter is foamy and melted, use a slotted spoon to lift English muffins out of egg mixture and add them to the skillet, spreading out evenly; discard any remaining egg mixture. Cook for 5 minutes or until deeply browned, then turn with a spatula, scraping if necessary to release the English muffins from the pan and breaking apart the larger clumps. Cook for about 4 minutes longer or until the second side is well browned. Transfer English muffins to a serving bowl. Drizzle syrup over English muffins, stirring to distribute evenly. Add berries and stir gently to combine. Serve immediately. ◊

NORTHLAND SWEET SAUSAGE GRAVY AND BISCUITS

Traditional southern sausage gravy is delicious but very rich. This version, while not exactly diet food, is lightened somewhat by the addition of onions and apples; a shot of maple syrup provides extra sweetness. If you prefer, serve the sausage gravy over hot, cooked grits. **SERVES 4**

- 6 ounces bulk pork breakfast sausage
- 1 cup whole milk
- ½ cup chicken broth (or milk, for a more traditional gravy)
- 2½ tablespoons maple syrup
- ¼–½ teaspoon hot pepper sauce, optional
- butter or vegetable oil if needed
- ⅓ cup finely chopped onion
- ½ small apple, peeled, cored, and finely chopped (¼–⅓ cup)
- 2½ tablespoons all-purpose flour
- ¼ teaspoon freshly ground black pepper
- 4 hot buttermilk biscuits, split

\>>

In large skillet, cook sausage over medium heat until browned and fully cooked, stirring and breaking up into small crumbles with a wooden spatula or spoon. While sausage is cooking, stir together milk, broth (if using), syrup, and hot pepper sauce in a measuring cup or bowl; set aside.

When sausage is done, use a slotted spoon to transfer it to a bowl; set aside. If there is more than 3 tablespoons of drippings in the skillet, drain and discard the excess; if there is less, add butter or vegetable oil to make up the difference. Add onion and apple to skillet and cook over medium heat, stirring frequently, until very tender, about 5 minutes. Sprinkle flour into skillet, stirring constantly. Cook for about a minute, stirring frequently. Slowly pour in milk mixture, stirring constantly. Cook until bubbly and beginning to thicken, about 3 minutes. Return sausage to skillet and add pepper; cook, stirring frequently, until the gravy is as thick as you like, a minute or two longer. Spoon over split-open biscuits. ◇

BOSTOCK: FRANGIPANE-TOPPED TOAST

I first encountered bostock *at Rustica, a wonderful bakery near Lake Calhoun in Minneapolis. After enjoying it there, I did some research and learned that bostock is a sweet pastry devised in France to use up stale brioche, a rich, buttery bread. The traditional version is prepared by dipping the stale bread in an almond- or orange-infused simple syrup, then topping it with an almond paste called* frangipane *and finishing with a scattering of sliced almonds. When the bostock are baked, the frangipane puffs slightly and develops a crisp crust, while the bread lightly caramelizes outside but remains moist inside. Hungry yet?*

This version uses a maple mixture to moisten the bread and also adds a hit of maple to the frangipane. Note: The frangipane needs to be prepared at least an hour in advance and can be stored in the refrigerator up to two days before using. This recipe is written for a fairly large loaf of bread, five to six inches across; if your loaf is smaller, you will end up with more pieces if you use all the topping. It's best to use a stale portion of a loaf, but you can also set slices on the counter for an hour or two to dry them out before using them. **MAKES ABOUT 8 LARGE PIECES, DEPENDING ON THE SIZE OF THE BREAD**

1 cup slivered almonds (about 3¾ ounces)

⅓ cup sugar

2 tablespoons all-purpose flour

pinch salt

7 tablespoons unsalted butter, softened, cut into 7 chunks

2 eggs, at room temperature

3 tablespoons plus ½ cup maple syrup, divided

8 large slices stale brioche, challah, or other high-quality rich bread (see head note), cut ¾ to 1 inch thick

⅓ cup water

1 teaspoon vanilla extract

½–¾ cup sliced almonds

powdered sugar for dusting

....

Combine almonds, sugar, flour, and salt in a food processor and process until very fine. Add butter, eggs, and 3 tablespoons syrup to almond mixture. Process until smooth and pasty, 30 seconds to 1 minute, scraping the sides with a rubber spatula once. Scrape the almond paste into a bowl; cover and refrigerate at least 1 hour or as long as 2 days.

When you're ready to bake, heat oven to 400 degrees and generously coat a baking sheet with cooking spray. Place bread on prepared baking sheet. In a small bowl, stir together ½ cup syrup with the water and vanilla. Use a pastry brush to coat the bread with the maple dip: brush the top side twice, letting it soak in between each brushing, then turn and repeat on the second side. The bread should be moist but not soggy. Spoon some of the frangipane over the top side, using enough to make a layer that is about ¼ inch thick; use a table knife and clean fingers to spread it to cover the bread all the way to the crust. Sprinkle sliced almonds over the frangipane. Bake until the edges of the bread are browned, the frangipane is golden brown and lightly puffed, and almonds are lightly toasted, 15 to 20 minutes. Remove from oven and dust with powdered sugar. Let stand on baking sheet for 10 minutes, then loosen with a spatula and transfer to a wire rack. Serve warm or at room temperature. The slices can be cut in half for smaller servings if you like; it's very rich. ◇

Maple-Caramel Overnight Rolls

I learned this method of making caramel rolls from my mother-in-law, Bernita Bohnenstingl, who has prepared them for many years for bake sales and church functions in her rural western Minnesota community. Her caramel is made from a blend of heavy cream and brown sugar; my version substitutes butter for the cream and includes a generous pour of maple syrup. Assemble the rolls the evening before you want to serve them; the next morning, you can have fresh, warm rolls on the table in about two hours. I use my bread machine to mix and rise—but not bake—a basic white bread dough. If you prefer, mix and knead the dough in the traditional manner and let it rise once, then punch it down before using in this recipe. (Bernita uses a thawed one-pound loaf of frozen bread dough to make preparation easier—and you can, too.) Note: Before beginning, please read "Reducing Maple Syrup" on page 14 and "Testing a Thermometer" on page 16. **MAKES 9 ROLLS**

DOUGH

2 tablespoons maple syrup

approximately ⅞ cup cold water

1 egg

2½ cups bread flour

1 tablespoon unsalted butter, melted and cooled slightly

1½ teaspoons quick-rise yeast

1 teaspoon salt

⅔ cup maple syrup

5½ tablespoons unsalted butter, divided
(1½ tablespoons need to be softened)

2 tablespoons light brown sugar

½ teaspoon vanilla extract

up to ½ cup maple sugar crystals (see page 14)
or ½ cup chopped pecans, optional

1 tablespoon white sugar

1 teaspoon cinnamon

⅛ teaspoon nutmeg

....

Prepare the dough (use a standard or large-capacity bread machine; you may also prepare the dough by hand, following the standard procedure for yeast breads): Add 2 tablespoons syrup to two-cup measure, then add cold water to equal 1 cup. Add egg to measuring cup with maple mixture and beat with a fork until combined. Add maple mixture and all remaining dough ingredients to bread machine according to instructions for your machine. (Some have special yeast dispensers and require the liquids to be added last, on top of the flour; others require the liquid to be added first so it is at the bottom of the mixing pan, with the yeast on top of the flour.) Run the white dough cycle so the dough is kneaded and proofed; watch the dough in the first few minutes of kneading and add a little more water (or flour) if the dough appears too dry (or too wet).

When dough cycle is complete (or, if making dough by hand, when it has risen once and been punched down), turn dough out onto a lightly floured work surface and knead a few times. Pat into a rough rectangle about an inch thick, then cover loosely with a towel and let it rest while you prepare the caramel topping. Coat a 9x9–inch baking dish with cooking spray; set aside.

To prepare the caramel topping, place ⅔ cup syrup in a heavy-bottomed small saucepan. Heat over medium heat until the surface is covered with foaming bubbles, then adjust heat so mixture continues to bubble but does not boil over and cook, stirring frequently, until it reaches 23 degrees above boiling on a tested quick-read thermometer (see head note;

>>

235 degrees if your thermometer measures boiling water at 212 degrees); this will probably take 3 to 5 minutes from the time the mixture starts boiling. Remove from heat and add 4 tablespoons butter; stir constantly until butter is completely melted. Add brown sugar and vanilla and stir until completely smooth, then pour into prepared baking dish; scatter sugar crystals or pecans (if using) over the mixture. Set aside to cool slightly while you roll out the dough.

Uncover the dough and roll it into a rectangle that is about 9 by 14 inches. Spread 1½ tablespoons softened butter over the dough. Stir together the white sugar, cinnamon, and nutmeg in a small bowl; sprinkle evenly over the buttered dough. Starting with one long edge, roll firmly into a log. Pinch the edge together very well to seal, and pat the ends in slightly if necessary so the log is about 13½ inches long. Cut the log into 9 pieces, each about 1½ inches wide. Arrange rolls, cut-side up, in the baking dish on top of the maple mixture. Cover dish with foil that has been lightly coated with cooking spray and refrigerate overnight.

The next morning, place the covered rolls on the counter and let stand at room temperature for 1 to 2 hours; the longer time is slightly better. Near the end of the standing time, heat oven to 350 degrees for a glass dish or 375 degrees for a metal pan. Uncover the rolls and bake in the center of the oven for 35 to 40 minutes, checking after about 20 minutes and covering dish loosely with foil if rolls are browning too quickly. The rolls are done when the caramel is bubbling vigorously, the tops are richly browned, and the rolls feel springy, not mushy, when pressed with a fingertip. Remove from oven and remove foil if used; let stand for 3 or 4 minutes. Run a table knife around the edges of the dish to loosen the rolls if it seems necessary, then cover dish with foil, using a pot holder to fold it gently down the sides. Lay a platter on top of the foil-covered dish. Grasp the dish and platter together firmly with pot holders, then carefully but quickly flip them over together and place on the counter. Make sure the foil is still wrapped up along the sides of the dish to catch any caramel that might spill out. Let stand for about 30 seconds, then carefully lift off the baking dish. Use a large spoon to scoop any remaining caramel from the dish, spooning it over the rolls. Let the rolls cool for at least 20 minutes before serving. ◊

Apple Pie Oatmeal with Maple

If you like to eat leftover apple pie or apple crisp for breakfast, you'll enjoy this dish. It's got the apple flavor you love, and it's a much healthier choice! If you like, add a few tablespoons of raisins or dried cranberries to the mixture along with the oats. **SERVES 2**

- ¼ cup maple syrup, plus additional for serving
- 1 tablespoon unsalted butter
- 1 teaspoon vanilla extract
- ¾ teaspoon cinnamon
- ¼ teaspoon nutmeg
- 1 Granny Smith or other tart apple, peeled, cored, and cut into ½-inch chunks (about 1½ cups)
- 1½ cups water
- ⅛ teaspoon salt
- 1 cup old-fashioned rolled oats
- 2 tablespoons chopped pecans or walnuts, optional
- milk or half-and-half for serving, optional

In a heavy-bottomed medium saucepan, stir together ¼ cup syrup, butter, vanilla, cinnamon, and nutmeg. Heat to boiling over medium-high heat and cook, stirring constantly, for about 1 minute. Add apple chunks; reduce heat to medium and cook, stirring frequently, for 5 to 6 minutes, until apples are beginning to soften. Add water and salt; heat to boiling. Stirring constantly, add oats in a steady stream. Adjust heat so mixture boils gently and cook for 5 minutes, stirring frequently, especially near the end of cooking time. Divide between two bowls; sprinkle each with half of the chopped nuts (if using). Serve with milk and additional syrup. ◊

NORTH WOODS EGGS BENEDICT

Orange juice and maple syrup put an interesting spin on classic hollandaise sauce. Rather than the more complicated poached eggs typically used in eggs Benedict, over-easy eggs seem appropriate to the informal north woods setting, but if you prefer to make poached eggs, they'll work fine here. For an interesting variation, substitute sliced Serrano ham for the Canadian-style bacon; I've also substituted flaked, smoked salmon. Note: If you use the smaller amount of sauce on each serving, you'll have leftover sauce, so you could prepare enough of the other ingredients for six servings if you like. You can also store leftover sauce in the refrigerator for a day or two and re-warm in the microwave on low power before serving; it's good on cooked broccoli or asparagus. **SERVES 4**

....

NORTH WOODS HOLLANDAISE

- 4 egg yolks
- 2 tablespoons maple syrup
- 1 tablespoon freshly squeezed orange juice
- ¼ teaspoon dry mustard
- ⅛–¼ teaspoon salt, to taste
- ¾ cup (1½ sticks) unsalted butter, melted and cooled slightly

- 4 English muffins, split
- unsalted butter as needed (about 2 tablespoons total)
- 4 ounces sliced Canadian-style bacon
- 4 whole eggs

....

Heat oven to 250 degrees. Prepare the north woods hollandaise: Fill a large skillet halfway with cold water and add a few ice cubes; set aside. Combine egg yolks, syrup, orange juice, mustard, and salt in a heavy-bottomed medium saucepan; whisk until blended. Add melted butter, whisking constantly. Cook over medium-low heat, whisking constantly and being sure to get into the corners of the pan, until the mixture thickens, 2½ to 4 minutes: don't overcook or the eggs will begin to scramble. Set the saucepan in the skillet of cold water and continue to whisk for about a minute longer; this step prevents the mixture from overcooking. Remove the saucepan from the cold water. Drain the skillet and fill it halfway with very hot tap water. Place the covered saucepan back into it to keep the sauce warm until you're ready to serve.

Toast the English muffins, buttering them lightly and placing them on a plate in the oven as they are done to keep them warm. Melt a little butter in a large skillet and fry the Canadian-style bacon on both sides until hot; keep warm in oven while you fry the eggs. Melt a tablespoon or so of butter in the same skillet, then carefully crack the eggs into the skillet, keeping them separated as much as possible (a griddle works better for this, so if you have one, use it instead of the skillet). Cook until the bottom side is firm and the runny edges around the yolk are starting to firm up, then carefully flip each egg and cook 30 to 45 seconds longer; the yolk should still be runny.

Without delay, put one English muffin half on each plate and top with one-quarter of the Canadian-style bacon. Gently lay a fried egg on each of the bacon-topped English muffin halves. Pour 2 to 3½ tablespoons of the warm north woods hollandaise over each egg (see head note), then set each remaining English muffin half at an angle, partly covering the egg. Serve immediately. ◇

CANDIED BACON

Candied bacon is a fairly recent "blogosphere phenomenon" that is usually made with brown sugar. Maple syrup is even better, taking this decadent but simple preparation to another level. The recipe is written for half a pound of bacon, but it's easy to change the amount since the preparation is so simple. You might want to make extra and use the cooled, crumbled candied bacon to top ice cream, stir into muffin batter, add to sandwiches or burgers, mix in with cookie dough (especially for chocolate chip cookies), or sprinkle over salad or thick soup. **SERVES 4**

½ pound thick-sliced bacon (8–9 slices)

⅓ cup maple syrup

Position oven rack in center of oven, and heat to 400 degrees. Line a large rimmed baking sheet with foil, bringing it up at the sides to form a lip, then place a wire cooling rack on the lined sheet. Arrange bacon in a single layer on the rack, keeping slices separate. Bake for 10 minutes, then remove from oven and use tongs to turn bacon over. Use a pastry brush to dab syrup liberally over the bacon, using about one-third of the syrup. Bake for 7 minutes, then remove from oven. Use tongs to turn the bacon; brush the bacon with half of the remaining syrup. Return to oven and bake for 7 minutes, then remove, turn the bacon, and brush with remaining syrup. Return to oven and bake for 4 to 7 minutes longer, until edges are crisp and bacon looks glazed. Remove from oven and let stand for about 3 minutes to allow the glaze to set, then transfer bacon to a serving plate. (If you don't remove the bacon after a few minutes, it will stick to the rack—and don't even think about lining the serving plate with paper towels!) Serve immediately; refrigerate leftovers.

Variations: If you care to gild the lily further, try one of these variations.

- Whisk about ½ teaspoon Dijon mustard and ⅛ teaspoon cayenne pepper, black pepper, or chili powder into the maple syrup before using.

- Use pepper-coated bacon instead of plain bacon.

- At the end of cooking, when the bacon has been removed from the oven, sprinkle some mini chocolate chips over the bacon, then use a table knife to spread it after it melts in a minute or two.

- Stir together 3 tablespoons finely chopped pecans and 1 tablespoon brown sugar. For the first step, cook bacon for 7 minutes rather than 10; remove from oven, brush with maple syrup as directed, and cook for 7 minutes. Remove from oven, brush with remaining maple syrup, and sprinkle nut/sugar mixture evenly over the bacon. Return to oven and bake for 10 minutes longer or until bacon is crisp and the topping is bubbling. ◇

Breakfast Smoothies with Maple

Smoothies are a snap to whip up in the morning and can be easily varied to suit the ingredients you have on hand. I always use half a banana to provide body, but if you don't care for bananas you can substitute half an apple. Here are a few smoothie combinations I enjoy; experiment to find your own favorite. **SERVES 2**

....

MANGO-MAPLE SMOOTHIE

1½ cups vanilla soy milk

1 cup diced fresh mango (about ½ mango)

½ cup plain yogurt

3 tablespoons maple syrup

½ medium banana

ORANGE-MAPLE SMOOTHIE

1½ cups freshly squeezed orange juice

1 cup frozen raspberries

2 scoops vanilla frozen yogurt

3 tablespoons maple syrup

½ medium banana

PEACH-MAPLE SMOOTHIE WITH FLAX SEEDS

1½ cups almond milk

½ cup frozen peach slices

½ cup frozen strawberries or raspberries

3 tablespoons maple syrup

1 tablespoon ground flax seeds

½ medium banana

....

Combine all ingredients in blender; for additional body, add several ice cubes. Pulse a few times, then run steadily until mixture is smooth. Pour into two tall glasses and serve immediately. ◇

Homemade
Specialties

T his chapter highlights maple's versatility in preparing some food basics that are primarily used as ingredients in various recipes or as accompaniments to other dishes. Most keep very well and can be pulled out of the fridge, freezer, or pantry whenever you want to add a touch of maple to almost any meal.

HOME-SMOKED MAPLE BACON

Traditionally, bacon is prepared by brining pork belly—or sometimes jowl—in a mixture of salt and sugar and then smoking it at temperatures below 100 degrees. Smoking at this temperature is called cold-smoking. *Because dangerous bacteria can thrive at these low temperatures, preservatives including sodium nitrate and sodium nitrite are traditionally added to the mixture. Meats that have been prepared with these preservatives are referred to as* cured. *Due to the preservatives, the meaty portions in cured bacon have an appealing pink color, and the bacon can be safely kept for several weeks in the refrigerator even though it is uncooked.*

Recent health concerns about these preservatives, however, have started a movement toward uncured bacon and other smoked meats. Many experts suggest that amateurs should not cold-smoke uncured meats due to the possibility of bacteria growth. Generally, a cooking temperature of 160 degrees or higher is considered safe for home-smoking uncured meats.

Happily, bacon comes out quite nicely when smoke-cooked at 175 to 225 degrees, similar to the temperature range used for traditional low-and-slow barbecue cooking. A covered grill works fine for this technique, although it takes a bit of fiddling to maintain the grill at the proper temperature. The finished bacon is nicely smoked—and fully cooked—after two to three hours, typically. The meaty portions will be grayish-brown rather than pink, and since no preservatives are included you'll need to freeze any amount you won't be using within a few days.

You'll need a few special supplies. First up is a chunk of raw pork belly (also called side pork), which is becoming easier to locate as this cut finds its way onto menus at high-end restaurants. Look for it at a full-service butcher; co-ops may also carry it. Another option is to visit an Asian or Mexican market; these cultures have been cooking pork belly since long before it became trendy, and a good market is likely to have it. It's typically sold in one-and-a-half- to two-pound chunks and may be skin on or skinless. I prefer skinless pork belly because I think it absorbs the flavorings and smoke better, but skin on will also work. Look for a piece of pork belly that has thick layers of meat; sometimes it seems to be mostly fat, so it pays to dig through the freezer case or have the butcher show you more than one chunk.

For smoke-cooking, use natural lump charcoal rather than manufactured briquettes, which are laced with petroleum products that give the bacon a bad taste. Natural charcoal burns hotter and faster than manufactured briquettes, so you'll need to monitor the temperature frequently. Note that you'll be topping off the burning coals with fresh, unstarted coals throughout the procedure; natural charcoal ignites more quickly than manufactured briquettes and doesn't emit any noxious fumes, so you don't have to start the fresh charcoal in a separate grill. Natural charcoal chunks are typically unevenly sized. I like to start the fire with large chunks and then use a mix of large and small chunks when topping up the already-burning fire throughout the smoke-cooking.

Finally, you'll need some smoking-wood chunks. If you've got any maple, nut, or fruit trees in your yard, gather a few fallen branches and cut or break them up into three- to four-inch-long pieces. Ideally, the branches will be an inch or less in thickness; if they're thicker, use a saw to cut inch-thick circles and then saw or chop those into smaller pieces. You can also buy smoking-wood chunks from a sporting-goods store or larger supermarket. Hickory is easiest to find and works fine, but any species will do as long as it is packaged specifically for smoking. For the technique below, be sure to buy chunks, not sawdust or fine chips.

>>

To monitor the cooking temperature, I place an oven thermometer on the grate right next to the pork. Thermometers in the grill lid measure the temperature at the top of the grill, which can be considerably warmer than the temperature on the cooking grate; even a probe-style thermometer placed in a vent hole, with the tip of the probe several inches below the lid, may read 20 degrees (or more) warmer than the actual temperature on the grate. I have an oven thermometer dedicated to smoking; the metal parts darken after a few uses and periodically I have to clean the glass face with a scraping razor because it gets too dark to see the dial.

During the smoke-cooking, you will be adding fresh charcoal and smoking-wood chunks to already-burning coals. Some grill cooking grates have a hinged area that flips open so you can do this without taking off the whole grate. If you don't have a hinged grate, you'll have to pick up the whole grate to toss charcoal and wood on the burning coals; position the grate so the handles are not directly above the coals to make this step easier. It's helpful to have an assistant: one person lifts the grate while the other adds fresh charcoal and wood. You could also rig up something to set the grate on while you add the fresh material—a clean, open garbage can or second grill (unlit and open) works well.

Preparation begins a day—or more—in advance, so plan accordingly. The recipe is written for two pounds of pork belly; if you want to prepare more, simply increase the syrup and salt proportionally. (Thanks to Brett Laidlaw, whose recipe in his book, Trout Caviar, reminded me how easy it is to make homemade, smoke-cooked bacon.) **MAKES 1–2 POUNDS**

½ cup maple syrup

3 tablespoons kosher salt

1–2 small slabs or squares fresh pork belly (1½–2 pounds total), skinless or skin on

disposable 11x7–inch or 9x9–inch foil pan (you can reuse it several times)

natural lump charcoal (about 4 quarts; see above)

smoking-wood chunks (see above)

In measuring cup or bowl, stir together the syrup and salt; the salt won't dissolve completely. Use a metal skewer to poke holes at 1-inch intervals all over both sides of the pork belly. Place the pork in a zipper-style plastic food-storage bag that holds it comfortably. Scrape the syrup mixture into the bag. Seal the bag, pushing out as much air as possible, then place it in a sink full of cold water with the closure sticking out of the water. Open a corner of the bag: the water will press the plastic against the pork, pushing out the air, so all you need to do is submerge the bag almost completely and press out the rest of the air at the top. Reseal the bag and place it in a baking dish. Refrigerate for at least 24 hours and up to 3 days, turning the bag over and slightly massaging the syrup mixture into the pork (through the bag) several times each day.

When you're ready to smoke, set the foil pan on the coal grate (or on the bottom of the grill, if your grill doesn't have a coal grate), positioning it as close to the side as possible rather than in the center. Start about 1½ cups of larger charcoal chunks in a chimney starter, using newspaper (don't use lighter fluid; if you don't have a chimney starter, set some crumpled newspaper in the foil pan and arrange coals on that, then light the newspaper to start the coals).

When coals are covered with ash, pour them into the foil pan and push them together into a loose pile. Place the cooking grate in the grill and position an oven thermometer on the opposite side of the grate from the fire (so the thermometer is above an area with no coals). Cover the grill

>>

and check the temperature in 5 minutes. If the temperature is between 200 and 225 degrees, all is well. If it is hotter than that, remove a few coals (place them into a metal can or a second grill, if you have one); if it is cooler, add a few small chunks of unlit charcoal and check again in 10 minutes or so.

Once the temperature is between 200 and 225 degrees, rinse the pork very well in cold water and pat completely dry. Add a small handful of smoking-wood pieces to the ash-covered coals. Place the pork on the cooking grate on the side away from the coals, near the thermometer. If you're smoking more than one piece, arrange them in a single layer if possible while still keeping them away from the coals; if you need to stack pieces, angle the top ones so there is air space between all of them (rather than laying one piece flat atop another). Cover the grill so the top vent is positioned over the pork, then open the vent. Cook for 15 minutes, then check the temperature. If it is below 190 degrees, add a few large pieces of charcoal and a few smaller ones; if it has crept above 225 degrees, remove a few coals or spread them out a bit to break up the heat.

Re-cover the grill and continue to check the temperature every 30 minutes, adding more coals when necessary to maintain the temperature between 175 and 225 degrees. Also add a few more pieces of smoking-wood every half hour (or as needed), and flip the pork over with tongs, orienting it so the side that was toward the coals is now facing the outside of the grill. After about 2 hours, check the temperature of the pork with a quick-read thermometer; it needs to reach 160 degrees. If necessary, continue smoke-cooking, checking the pork every half hour, until the pork reaches 160 degrees (usually 2 to 3 hours total).

Cool the bacon before wrapping and storing in the refrigerator; for storage beyond a few days, cut the bacon into smaller chunks (½ pound or so), wrap tightly, and freeze until needed. To serve, slice as thick or thin as you like, and fry over low heat until crisp. ◊

Chipotle-Maple Barbecue Sauce

Chipotle peppers are smoked jalapeños; they offer both heat and a deep, smoky flavor. They marry well with the sweet maple syrup in this rich barbecue sauce. Frying the dry spices before adding the wet ingredients helps the flavors "bloom." Note: One teaspoon of chipotle powder makes a nicely balanced sauce with enough kick to notice but not overpower. If you like a really spicy barbecue sauce, use up to two teaspoons of chipotle powder. Look for chipotle powder, ancho powder, and smoked Spanish paprika at Penzeys. **MAKES ABOUT 2 CUPS**

½ cup finely chopped onion

1½ tablespoons vegetable oil

2 cloves garlic, pressed or minced

2 teaspoons smoked Spanish paprika (sweet, not hot)

1–2 teaspoons chipotle chile powder (see head note)

1 teaspoon ancho chile powder

½ teaspoon cumin

½ teaspoon freshly ground black pepper

1 (15-ounce) can (or about 1½ cups) crushed tomatoes

¾ cup maple syrup

¼ cup cider vinegar

1 tablespoon prepared yellow mustard

1 tablespoon Worcestershire sauce

In a heavy-bottomed medium saucepan, cook onion in oil over medium-low heat until tender crisp, about 4 minutes, stirring frequently. Add garlic and cook for about 30 seconds longer. Stir in paprika, chipotle powder, ancho powder, cumin, and black pepper. Continue to cook, stirring constantly, for about 30 seconds longer (it's a good idea to turn on

>>

the vent fan while you're cooking the dry spices). Add remaining ingredients, stirring well. Adjust heat so mixture is bubbling very gently and cook, stirring frequently, for about 25 minutes, adjusting heat as needed to maintain a very gentle bubbling. Cool and transfer to a clean jar. The sauce can be used the day you make it, but it's a bit better if refrigerated for at least a day, allowing the flavors to mellow and blend. The barbecue sauce will keep for a month in the refrigerator. ◇

HOMEMADE GRANOLA

A friend brought me a bag of granola from The Bread Barn in Madison, Wisconsin, and it was the best I'd ever had. I couldn't find a place to buy it locally, so I studied the label on the bag and came up with my own version, tailoring the ingredients to my taste; the maple, almond extract, and combination of various nuts seem to be key to the outstanding flavor. I store the granola in one-quart canning jars in the cupboard; I expect it keeps for a very long time, but it never lasts more than a month around our house because it is so good. Note: Raw or roasted nuts both work in this recipe, and if roasted they can be salted or unsalted, according to your taste and what you have in the pantry. **MAKES ABOUT 5½ CUPS**

DRY INGREDIENTS

- 3 cups old-fashioned rolled oats
- ½ cup wheat germ
- ⅓ cup pistachios (about 1½ ounces), cut in halves or thirds before measuring
- ¼ cup unflavored pumpkin seeds (pepitas)
- ¼ cup chopped pecans (about 1 ounce)
- ¼ cup broken cashews (about 1¼ ounces)
- ¼ cup unsweetened coconut flakes, optional
- 2 tablespoons very coarsely ground flax seeds

GLAZE

¼ cup vegetable oil

½ cup maple syrup

⅓ cup packed light brown sugar

1 tablespoon butter

¼ teaspoon almond extract

....

Heat oven to 350 degrees. Coat a 10x15–inch jelly roll pan with cooking spray; set aside. Combine dry ingredients in very large mixing bowl; stir well and set aside. Combine glaze ingredients in a medium microwave-safe mixing bowl. Microwave on high for 2½ minutes; remove and stir until mixture is smooth. Pour over dry ingredients, stirring very well to coat. Spread on prepared jelly roll pan. Bake until golden brown and no longer wet-looking, about 25 minutes, removing from oven and stirring thoroughly every 6 or 7 minutes; be careful not to over-brown. Cool on baking sheet, then transfer to glass jars for storage. ◇

Apple-Maple Leather

You need a dehydrator to make this delicious fruit roll-up, which is a great snack to toss in a backpack when you're heading out on a hike. Smaller pieces can be wrapped in waxed paper and tucked into a school or office lunch box, too. This recipe makes one leather, but to get more out of the lengthy dehydrating process you might want to prepare an additional batch or two as soon as the first one has been started in the dehydrator (it's easier to make one batch of purée at a time rather than a double batch, which is a bit too much for easy processing). The leather can be stored at room temperature, but it will retain its flavor better over longer periods if kept in the refrigerator or freezer. **MAKES 1 (12-INCH-WIDE) LEATHER**

1½ pounds apples (3 large or 4 medium), peeled, cored, and cut into ¾-inch chunks

¼ cup maple syrup, preferably grade B

1 tablespoon orange juice or lemon juice

½ teaspoon vanilla extract

Coat a solid liner sheet from a dehydrator with cooking spray; place on the dehydrator tray and set aside. Combine all ingredients in a large microwave-safe bowl and microwave on high, stirring every 2 minutes, until all apple chunks are very tender, about 11 minutes. (Alternatively, you may simmer the mixture in a covered saucepan for 8 to 10 minutes, stirring several times.) Let stand for 10 minutes, then transfer to food processor and process until very smooth, about 90 seconds, scraping down the sides as needed.

Scrape purée onto prepared dehydrator liner sheet. Use a rubber spatula to distribute the purée evenly and smooth the top; it should be about ¼ inch thick. Dehydrate at 130–40 degrees until leathery, with no sticky spots, about 6 to 10 hours, depending on your dehydrator, the weather, and the moisture content of the apples. For more even drying, flip the leather over once it is firm enough to pry off in a single piece and continue drying until done. When the leather is evenly dry on both sides and is leathery, peel it off the liner sheet and lay it on a sheet of plastic wrap; let cool for a few minutes, then roll up the plastic wrap and leather together.

Variation: Oven-Dried Apple-Maple Leather

If your oven can be set to 150 degrees (or has a setting specifically for dehydrating, a feature found on some convection ovens), you can use it to dehydrate the leather. You'll need to prop the door open about 2 inches with a ball of foil to allow moisture to escape. If your oven has a light that comes on whenever the door is open, either remove the bulb or disable the light by taping a small piece of wood over the switch. Use an oven thermometer to monitor the temperature. If the oven gets too warm, you can turn it off and let the leather continue to dry in the residual heat; alternate between on and off cycles to maintain the temperature.

Prepare the purée as directed above. Line a rimmed baking sheet with plastic wrap, taping the edges to the baking sheet on all sides to keep it in place during filling and drying. Pour prepared purée into the prepared, lined baking sheet; distribute purée evenly, about ¼ inch thick. Place in oven, propping door open as noted above. Dry until leathery, flipping once as noted above. Total drying time will be 6 to 12 hours. If the leather is partially dry but still a bit sticky when you're ready for bed, simply turn the oven off and leave the door propped open to allow the leather to continue to dry overnight; continue in the morning if necessary. ◊

CREAMY MAPLE BUTTER

This slightly soft, creamy butter is fabulous on toast, pancakes, or anything else you'd spread butter on. Note: If possible, use a European-style butter such as Plugrá or Lurpak, which has a higher butterfat content than regular butter and works better with the syrup because the extra fat helps keep the butter creamy, even with the addition of the liquid syrup. You'll need two clean half-pint canning jars to store the finished butter; I prefer the short, squat, wide-mouth shape for this recipe because it's easier to scoop out the finished butter. Before beginning, please read "Reducing Maple Syrup" on page 14 and "Testing a Thermometer" on page 16. **MAKES 2 HALF-PINT JARS**

1 cup maple syrup

1 cup (2 sticks) unsalted butter (see head note), cut into 4 pieces

Place syrup in a heavy-bottomed medium saucepan. Cook over medium heat without stirring until the surface is covered with foaming bubbles. Boil without stirring until mixture reaches 22 degrees above boiling on a tested quick-read thermometer (see head note; 234 degrees if your thermometer measures boiling water at 212 degrees); this will probably take 8 to 12 minutes from the time the mixture starts boiling. Remove from heat; drop in the butter and stir constantly until the butter melts completely. Continue stirring for about 2 minutes longer. Pour into two half-pint canning jars; seal tightly. The butter will keep in the refrigerator for several weeks or in the freezer for several months.

Variation: Whipped Maple Butter

Commercially prepared maple butter is often whipped, which increases the volume slightly and makes the butter look more pale. If you want whipped maple butter, place it in a mixing bowl rather than pouring it into the canning jars, and then beat with an electric mixer on medium-high speed for about 5 minutes, until the color lightens. Scrape into jars, seal tightly, and refrigerate or freeze. It may crystallize somewhat after being refrigerated. ◇

Sweet and Spicy Chile-Maple Dipping Sauce

You may have had a sweet, spicy dipping sauce at a Vietnamese or Thai restaurant, where it's often served with spring rolls and other appetizers. Here's a similar version you can make at home that combines the wonderful flavor of maple with spicy Sriracha hot pepper sauce (an Asian-style condiment made in California by Huy Fong Foods, also called "rooster sauce" because the bottle bears an illustration of a large, strutting rooster) and dark sesame oil. Look for Sriracha at Asian markets or in the Asian section at large, well-stocked supermarkets. Serve this sauce with egg rolls, fresh or fried spring rolls, chicken wings, grilled or deep-fried shrimp, and fried wontons—cream cheese wontons are a particularly good choice. **MAKES ABOUT ½ CUP**

⅓ cup maple syrup

1 tablespoon rice vinegar

2 teaspoons cold water

1 teaspoon dark sesame oil

1 teaspoon Sriracha hot pepper sauce (see head note), or to taste

1 tablespoon finely chopped unsalted dry-roasted peanuts

To prepare the sauce, combine syrup, vinegar, water, sesame oil, and Sriracha in a small mixing bowl, whisking to blend. Transfer to a small serving bowl; scatter peanuts over the top. Refrigerate any leftover sauce. ◇

Tavern-Style Maple Mustard

Homemade mustard is easy to make, especially when you soak the seeds before trying to break them up. Maple syrup adds a wonderful sweet note to this spicy mustard. Note: The mustard needs to be refrigerated for a full day before using to allow the flavor to mellow. If you taste it right after blending, it will be very harsh, but after twenty-four hours the flavor will be much more smooth and complex. **MAKES ABOUT 1 CUP**

¼ cup yellow mustard seeds

3 tablespoons brown mustard seeds

⅓ cup white wine vinegar

⅓ cup cold apple juice

⅓ cup maple syrup

¼ cup dry mustard

1 teaspoon kosher salt

In small nonaluminum mixing bowl, combine yellow mustard seeds, brown mustard seeds, vinegar, and apple juice; stir well. Cover with plastic wrap and let stand at room temperature for 18 to 24 hours, stirring once or twice in the first few hours.

After soaking, add mustard seed mixture to blender with syrup, dry mustard, and salt. Pulse a few times, then process on high until the texture is the way you prefer it (about 20 seconds will produce a somewhat coarse mustard with a thick base). Transfer to a glass jar and seal tightly; refrigerate for at least 24 hours before using (see head note). ◊

BLUEBERRY-WALNUT SYRUP

Hang on to your fork: this is not a simple blueberry-flavored syrup but rather a wonderful, chunky mix with fresh blueberries, buttery pan-toasted walnuts, and pure maple syrup. Use on pancakes, French toast, or waffles for a superlative breakfast; it's also great as a dessert sauce, spooned over ice cream or cake. **MAKES ABOUT 2 CUPS**

2 tablespoons unsalted butter

½ cup chopped walnuts (medium-fine; about 2 ounces)

1½ cups fresh blueberries

1½ cups maple syrup

½ teaspoon lemon juice

dash cinnamon

½ teaspoon cornstarch mixed with 1 teaspoon cold water

In a heavy-bottomed medium saucepan, melt butter over medium heat. When butter is foamy, add walnuts; cook, stirring frequently, until nuts begin to brown and smell toasty, 1½ to 2 minutes. Add blueberries, syrup, lemon juice, and cinnamon. Heat to boiling; adjust heat so mixture boils but does not boil over and cook for 15 minutes, stirring occasionally. Stir the cornstarch mixture again, then drizzle it into the syrup mixture, stirring constantly. Cook for about 2 minutes longer, then remove from heat and set aside for at least 10 minutes before serving. Serve warm if using with pancakes, French toast, or waffles; it's best at room temperature when used to top ice cream or cake. Refrigerate leftovers in a tightly sealed container; they'll keep for a week or longer. ◊

PORK AND MAPLE SAUSAGE

This delicious, slightly sweet sausage is fabulous when formed into patties and pan-fried for breakfast; it also works well in any recipe that uses breakfast-style sausage. You can chop the meat with either a good meat grinder or a food processor. A meat grinder does a much better job of cutting up any stringy bits of meat and produces a more consistent texture.

MAKES 2 POUNDS

....

3	tablespoons maple syrup
1–1¼	teaspoons kosher salt, to taste
1	teaspoon crumbled dried sage, or 2 teaspoons minced fresh
1	teaspoon dried thyme
¾	teaspoon freshly ground black pepper
½	teaspoon dried marjoram
¼	teaspoon freshly ground nutmeg
¼	teaspoon red pepper flakes, or to taste
2	pounds boneless pork shoulder (also called pork butt)

....

In a large glass, ceramic, or stainless-steel mixing bowl, combine all ingredients except the pork and stir until thoroughly mixed; set aside. To prepare the pork, cut off and set aside any large areas of fat, such as the layer of fat on the outside of the roast (don't worry if there is some meat attached). Cut the rest of the meat into 1-inch cubes, adding them to the bowl with the syrup mixture as you go. Once all meat has been added, stir well to coat the meat with the syrup mixture and cover bowl tightly with plastic wrap. Cut the fatty portions into ½-inch cubes; place in another bowl and cover with plastic wrap. Refrigerate the meat and fat at least 12 hours and as long as 24 hours, stirring the meat and syrup mixture once or twice.

If using a meat grinder: When you're ready to process the meat, put the medium plate (³⁄₁₆- or ¼-inch holes) in the grinder. Process the fat cubes through the grinder into a small bowl, then place in the freezer for 15 minutes. While the fat is chilling, grind the seasoned meat cubes through the medium plate, collecting the ground meat in a flat baking dish; refrigerate until needed. Remove the medium plate and place in the refrigerator to keep it cold, then put the fine plate (⅛-inch holes) in the grinder. When the fat has been in the freezer for 15 minutes, position the baking dish with the ground meat under the grinder and grind the fat into the dish. Use your hands to mix the ground meat and fat together very well. Place in the freezer for 15 minutes. Meanwhile, clean the grinder a bit and put the medium plate back in. Grind the combined mixture through the medium plate.

If using a food processor: Place the fat cubes in the work bowl with the steel blade and pulse a few times, then run the machine steadily until the mixture is very fine, about 10 to 15 seconds. Scrape the fat away from the sides and loosen it from the bottom of the work bowl with a rubber spatula. Add the seasoned meat, along with any liquid, to the fat and pulse until the meat is the texture you prefer, generally 8 to 10 pulses. Transfer the meat back into the mixing bowl and pick through it with your fingers, pulling out and discarding any stringy bits that didn't get chopped. If you find a few larger chunks, add them back to the food processor and chop them, then return to the bowl. If the mixture looks like it isn't evenly combined, mix it with your hands.

Divide the sausage mixture into half-pound portions or however you would like to store it. Pack into freezer-weight zipper-style bags, pressing the meat into the bottom of the bag and then rolling it up to force out any air before closing the zipper. (Or use a vacuum-sealing system if available.) The sausage can be shaped into flat patties and fried in a little oil over medium-low heat as a breakfast dish; it also can be used in any dish that calls for bulk sausage. ◇

snacks *and* APPETIZERS

opcorn! Peanuts! Chicken wings! Although this may sound like the cry of a vendor at the ballpark, it's a sneak peek at some of the recipes in this chapter. You'll also find party-worthy fare including a delicious yet simple stuffed date recipe with its roots in Spanish tapas, some outrageously good appetizers based on puff pastry, and an Italian-style crostini with a jammy topping—all featuring maple's smoky sweetness.

Two-Pepper Maple Chicken Wings

Sticky and gooey on the outside, with pull-off-the-bone tender meat. Serve these with cold beer—and plenty of napkins. **SERVES 6 AS AN APPETIZER**

2½	pounds chicken drumettes or jointed wings
1	teaspoon whole black peppercorns
1	teaspoon whole Szechuan peppercorns
⅔	cup maple syrup
2	tablespoons soy sauce
1½	tablespoons olive oil
1–2	cloves garlic, pressed or minced

Heat oven to 400 degrees for a glass dish or to 425 degrees for a metal pan. Line 13x9–inch baking dish with heavy-duty foil. Arrange chicken wings in dish; set aside.

With mortar and pestle, crush together the black and Szechuan pepper-corns until medium texture. Place in small mixing bowl. Add syrup, soy sauce, oil, and garlic; stir well to blend. Pour syrup mixture over chicken wings, tossing to coat. Bake until wings are tender and richly colored, 40 to 45 minutes, turning wings several times. Turn on broiler and cook wings until skin is crisped, about 10 minutes; turn wings several times during broiling and keep an eye on them so they don't burn. ◊

NEAR-BEER PEANUTS

These sweet-and-salty peanuts are somewhat similar to the famous Beer Nuts snack. Raw Spanish peanuts can be found in the supermarket alongside the nuts used for baking. **MAKES ABOUT 1 POUND**

2 teaspoons vegetable oil

1 pound raw Spanish peanuts (about 3¼ cups)

¾ cup maple syrup

¼ teaspoon salt, or to taste

Heat oven to 300 degrees. Line a large rimmed baking sheet with heavy-duty foil; brush oil over the foil and set aside. Combine peanuts and syrup in a heavy-bottomed large skillet and place over medium heat; be sure the pan is centered over the burner to prevent hot spots. Cook, stirring frequently with a wooden spoon, until liquid cooks away, 7 to 10 minutes. Reduce heat to medium-low and cook, stirring constantly, until the nuts begin to look sandy and are no longer glossy, 2 to 5 minutes. Scrape the mixture onto the prepared baking sheet, spreading evenly. Sprinkle lightly with some of the salt and stir to mix in the salt and oil. Bake for 15 minutes, then sprinkle lightly with salt and stir again; bake for 15 minutes longer or until the occasional nuts that have no skins—there are always one or two—are lightly browned. (While nuts are baking, fill the skillet with cold water and let it soak to loosen the crystallized maple sugar.)

When nuts are done, transfer baking sheet to a cooling rack and allow to cool completely. Don't sample a nut until they are completely cool; they are much hotter than you might expect when they first come out of the oven and will also be somewhat soft in texture until completely cool. Store in an airtight container at room temperature. ◊

BACON-WRAPPED DATES

I first encountered bacon-wrapped dates at Devotay, a wonderful Iowa City restaurant with many Spanish tapas-style items on the menu. Chef/ owner Kurt Michael Friese told me how to make them, and they have been a favorite of mine ever since. For the version below, I've added a double dose of maple; it's a fabulous complement to the dish. This recipe makes twenty appetizers, but it's so simple that you can easily adapt the quantities to suit your needs. Plan on at least two per person. Note: I use whole blanched almonds, but whole skin-on almonds would also work. For an extra-special touch, use whole Marcona almonds, which would be even more in keeping with the Spanish origins of the dish. **MAKES 20 APPETIZER-SIZE PORTIONS**

20 whole almonds (see head note)

¼ cup maple syrup, plus a bit more as needed

20 pitted dried dates (about 7 ounces)

10 slices regular bacon (about ½ pound; do not use thick-cut bacon)

Heat oven to 375 degrees. Place almonds in a small bowl; add ¼ cup syrup and stir to coat. Stuff one almond into each date, transferring them to a plate as you go. Cut the bacon slices into two shorter halves and arrange a few pieces on a small plate. Use a pastry brush to lightly coat both sides of the bacon pieces with the syrup remaining in the small bowl. Wrap a piece of maple-coated bacon firmly around a date, then place it on a broiler pan with the end of the bacon underneath. Repeat with all dates and bacon; you may need a bit more syrup. Bake until the bacon is crisp and nicely browned, about 35 minutes. Serve hot, warm, or at room temperature. ◊

Chocolate-Striped Maple Caramel Corn

This snack is outrageously good: sweet, crunchy, and buttery. The maple syrup and the two-chocolate drizzle elevate it beyond normal caramel corn. Use the biggest bowl you can find—preferably one that holds four quarts or more—to mix the popcorn with the caramel, or you won't have room to stir the popcorn and evenly distribute the caramel. This recipe is adapted from my book Abundantly Wild: Collecting and Cooking Wild Edibles in the Upper Midwest. *Note: Before beginning, please read "Reducing Maple Syrup" on page 14 and "Testing a Thermometer" on page 16.* **MAKES ABOUT 10 CUPS**

1 tablespoon vegetable oil

⅓ cup uncooked popcorn kernels

1¼ cups maple syrup

6 tablespoons (¾ stick) unsalted butter

½ teaspoon salt

3 tablespoons white chocolate morsels

3 tablespoons dark or milk chocolate morsels

Coat a very large mixing bowl with cooking spray; set aside. In medium saucepan, combine oil with a few popcorn kernels. Heat over medium heat until the kernels begin to pop, then add remaining popcorn and cover the saucepan. Cook, shaking constantly, until all kernels have popped. Transfer popped corn to prepared mixing bowl; set aside.

In a heavy-bottomed medium saucepan, combine syrup, butter, and salt; clip a tested candy thermometer to the side of the pan (see head note, or see tip on page 55 for a method that doesn't use a candy thermometer). Place pan over medium heat and cook, stirring occasionally, until butter melts. Cook without stirring until mixture reaches the hard-crack stage, 88 degrees above boiling (300 degrees if your thermometer measures boiling water at 212 degrees); swirl the mixture in the pan occasionally to keep it well mixed, and tilt the pan if necessary so the tip of the thermometer is well covered by the boiling mixture. It will take 15 to 20 minutes for the caramel to reach the proper stage. While the syrup mixture is cooking, coat a 10x15–inch jelly roll pan (or large rimmed baking sheet) and a wooden spoon with cooking spray.

When the mixture reaches the hard-crack stage, pour it in a medium stream over the popcorn, stirring constantly with the wooden spoon until well mixed. Immediately transfer the popcorn to the jelly roll pan, spreading it out with the wooden spoon.

Place the white chocolate morsels in a small microwave-safe bowl. Microwave at 70 percent power for 40 seconds, then stir with a teaspoon; the morsels will probably be softened but not yet melted. Return to microwave and cook for 15 seconds at 70 percent power and stir again; repeat until the mixture can be stirred smooth. Spoon the melted chocolate into the corner of a small freezer-weight plastic zipper bag. Cut a very tiny hole in the corner of the bag, then squeeze the melted chocolate into the corner and drizzle it over the caramel corn. Now add the dark or milk chocolate morsels to the same bowl; melt as you did with the white chocolate, stirring the mixture well to blend any remaining white chocolate with the dark or milk chocolate. Spoon the mixture into the other corner of the zipper bag, cut another tiny hole, and drizzle it over the caramel corn. Let the corn set up for at least 30 minutes; if the chocolate is still runny, transfer the clusters to a large container and refrigerate for 30 minutes to harden the chocolate. Once set, the caramel corn can be stored at room temperature.

Tip: To test the caramel mixture for the hard-crack stage without a thermometer, drop a bit of the boiling mixture into a bowl of cold water. When it is at the hard-crack stage, the mixture will form a hard, brittle thread that can be broken.

Variations

- For plain maple caramel corn, omit the chocolate morsels.
- For nutty maple caramel corn, add ¾ to 1 cup coarsely chopped nuts to the popcorn in the bowl before preparing the caramel. Cashews, walnuts, peanuts, pecans, or hickory nuts all work well. The nutty maple caramel corn can be drizzled with chocolate or enjoyed plain. ◇

CROSTINI WITH ONION-WALNUT JAM

Make a batch of this delicious onion-walnut jam and keep it in the fridge so you can whip together a batch of crostini if unexpected company comes by—or anytime you like. The jam-topped toasts are delicious on their own and are also a perfect canvas for additional toppings. A few are suggested below, but feel free to experiment. You can also combine toppings on one toast: try a slice of plum with a bit of crumbled blue cheese, or a chunk of smoked salmon with alfalfa-onion sprouts. Plan on two or three crostini per person as an appetizer (although I could eat a half dozen, myself!).

MAKES ABOUT 1 CUP JAM, ENOUGH FOR 20–24 CROSTINI

ONION-WALNUT JAM

- 3 tablespoons butter
- 2 cups chopped onion (about 2 medium onions)
- 3 tablespoons maple syrup, preferably grade B
- ¼ teaspoon crumbled dried thyme
- ¼ cup finely chopped walnuts (about 1 ounce)

FOR SERVING

crusty baguette, cut into ½-inch slices

extra-virgin olive oil as needed
   (about 1 tablespoon per 10 crostini)

additional toppings, optional (suggested amounts per toast):
   1 teaspoon crumbled blue or Roquefort cheese; thin wedge
   of ripe pluot, plum, or apricot; a good pinch of fine sprouts
   such as alfalfa, broccoli, or radish; 1-inch chunk of smoked
   salmon, prosciutto, or Serrano ham; small sliver of sharp
   cheese such as Cheddar or Gruyère; small piece of crisp
   bacon; a few drops Sriracha or other thick hot pepper sauce

Prepare the onion-walnut jam: In a heavy-bottomed medium saucepan, melt butter over medium heat. Add onion and cook, stirring frequently, until the liquid has cooked away and onions are beginning to brown, 6 to 10 minutes. Reduce heat to medium-low and stir in the syrup and thyme. Cook, stirring frequently, until onions are very soft and richly browned, about 10 minutes. Add walnuts; cook for about 2 minutes longer, then remove from heat and set aside until cool. Store in refrigerator for up to 2 weeks; bring back to room temperature before using.

When you're ready to assemble the crostini, heat oven to 375 degrees. Place baguette slices on a baking sheet and brush both sides very lightly with olive oil. Bake until the first side is lightly golden, 8 to 10 minutes, then turn over and bake until the second side is lightly golden. It will cook more quickly than the first side, so the total baking time will be 13 to 16 minutes. Spread about 1 teaspoon of the room-temperature onion-walnut jam over each crostini, adding a little more if it seems to need it; add any additional topping(s) you like. ◇

Individual Baked Brie-Pear Puffs

These are very rich: plan on two per person as an appetizer. **MAKES 12 PUFFS**

- 2 teaspoons unsalted butter
- 2 medium pears (¾–1 pound total), peeled, cored, and cut into ¼-inch cubes
- 2 tablespoons maple syrup
- ¼ teaspoon (scant) dried thyme leaves
- 1 teaspoon Dijon mustard
- 1 sheet puff pastry (half of a 17.3-ounce package), thawed
- 1 (8-ounce) wheel Brie (you'll use about one-quarter of it)

Heat oven to 400 degrees. Generously coat a 12-cup mini muffin tin with cooking spray; set aside. Melt butter in medium skillet over medium heat. Add pears and cook, stirring frequently, for 10 minutes; pears should be soft and beginning to brown. Stir in syrup and thyme. Cook, stirring frequently, about 5 minutes longer; syrup should be absorbed and pears should be golden brown. Remove from heat and stir in mustard; set aside to cool for 5 to 10 minutes while you prepare the pastry. (The pear mixture may be prepared a day or two in advance; refrigerate until needed.)

Unfold puff pastry sheet on lightly floured work surface. Push the seams together firmly, then roll the pastry to a 9x10–inch square. Cut into 12 pieces, each 3 by 2½ inches. Fit one piece into each muffin cup, pressing firmly into the edges of the cups; the corners of the pastry should point upward rather than overlap one another. Divide the pear mixture between the cups, about 1½ teaspoons each. Cut 12 (½-inch) cubes of Brie, placing one cube in each cup; reserve remaining Brie for another use. Bake for 15 minutes or until the pastry is puffed and brown and the cheese has melted. Cool slightly before serving; best served warm and fresh. ◊

soups, salads, and sandwiches

I f you're raising an eyebrow at the prospect of maple syrup in these types of dishes, read on to discover some truly delicious new ideas. You may be surprised to learn that maple syrup pairs very well with some nontraditional partners, including cabbage, split peas, carrots, and escarole.

CANADIAN YELLOW SPLIT PEA SOUP

What makes this split pea soup Canadian, you might ask? Well, the split peas are yellow rather than the more common green split peas. (I'm not sure why yellow split peas are traditional in Canadian split pea soup, but there you have it.) Also, maple syrup is added to the soup during cooking and again at the table, which is probably the more Canadian aspect. In Quebec, the split peas are usually cooked with a ham bone or salt pork, while in Newfoundland salted beef is used instead. The version here is vegetarian and relies on my secret ingredient to add savoriness: marmite, a thicker-than-molasses spread made from yeast. It's one of the better sources of umami, the so-called fifth flavor that is described as "savory." Look for marmite with the baking supplies in large, well-stocked supermarkets; it comes in a small, rounded brown jar. Marmite is very sticky; if you coat your measuring spoon with cooking spray first, the marmite will come out more easily. (For a non-vegetarian version that doesn't use marmite, see the variation below.)

SERVES 4–5

- ½ pound yellow split peas (about 1 heaping cup), picked through and rinsed
- 2 quarts water
- 1 bay leaf
- 1 large shallot, finely chopped
- 1 stalk celery, broken into 2 pieces
- 3 medium carrots, peeled

1 medium leek, root end trimmed

½ cup diced turnip (¼-inch dice; about ½ small turnip)

  2 tablespoons maple syrup, preferably grade B

  2 teaspoons marmite (see head note)

½ teaspoon crumbled dried savory leaves

½ teaspoon dried thyme

¼ teaspoon salt

¼ cup minced fresh parsley

  freshly ground black pepper

  grade A maple syrup for serving

....

In 1-gallon soup pot, combine split peas, water, bay leaf, shallot, and celery; break one of the carrots in half and add to the pot. Cut the bottom of the leek away from the greens at the point where the leaves begin to fan out; reserve the bottom part for later. Pull the leaves apart and rinse very well in cold running water, then cut each into two shorter pieces and add to soup pot. Place over medium-high heat and heat just to boiling, stirring once or twice. Adjust heat so mixture is simmering and cook, uncovered, for 45 minutes, stirring several times.

Near the end of the 45 minutes, cut the two reserved carrots into quarters vertically, then slice ¼ inch thick. Cut the greenish neck off the reserved leek bottom and discard it; quarter the white part vertically and then slice thinly. Use tongs to fish out and discard the bay leaf, celery, carrot pieces, and leek leaves from the soup pot. Add the cut-up carrot and sliced leek along with the turnip, 2 tablespoons syrup, marmite, savory, thyme, and salt. Stir and return to simmering, then cook until vegetables are tender and soup is somewhat thick, about 45 minutes. Just before serving, stir in the parsley and grind a generous amount of black pepper over the soup. Serve in soup plates, passing additional maple syrup at the table for diners to add as they wish.

Variation: For a stock-based soup, omit the marmite and salt. Substitute 1 quart chicken broth or vegetable broth for 1 quart of the water; you'll still need 1 quart of water. Proceed as directed. Top soup with crisp diced bacon. ◇

Roasted Carrot–Ginger Soup with Maple

The sweetness of maple is a perfect complement to the natural sweetness of roasted carrots in this delicious soup; ginger, scallions, and Szechuan pepper add delightful flavor notes. Serve as a first course or as a luncheon dish with a loaf of good, crusty bread and a green salad. **MAKES 4 FIRST-COURSE SERVINGS OR 2 MAIN-DISH SERVINGS**

....

  1 pound carrots, peeled

  1 tablespoon olive oil

 ¼ teaspoon salt

  3 tablespoons maple syrup

  6 scallions, root ends trimmed

1-inch piece fresh ginger, peeled

  2 cloves garlic

  1 tablespoon unsalted butter

  1 quart chicken or vegetable broth

large pinch ground Szechuan pepper

....

Heat oven to 425 degrees for a glass dish or 450 degrees for a metal pan. Cut carrots into ½-inch lengths; if any pieces are ½ inch across or thicker, also cut them in half vertically. Combine with oil in 13x9–inch baking dish, tossing to coat. Sprinkle with salt. Bake, uncovered, for 20 minutes, then add syrup, stirring well. Return to oven and bake 20 to 25 minutes longer or until beginning to brown, stirring once or twice.

While carrots are roasting, cut the dark green top portions off the scallions and set aside. Slice the white and pale green parts into thin rings; set aside separately from the green tops. Cut ginger into thin slices, then mince together with the garlic. Melt butter in 1-gallon soup pot over medium-low heat. Add sliced scallions (not the green tops) and minced ginger-garlic mixture. Cook for 3 minutes, stirring frequently. Add broth and Szechuan pepper. Increase heat to medium-high and heat to boiling, then adjust heat so mixture boils very gently and cook for 15 minutes. If the carrots aren't done roasting yet, reduce heat to low to keep the broth warm until carrots have browned.

Add browned carrots and pan juices to pot with scallion mixture. Cook at a gentle boil for 10 minutes or until carrots are very tender. Meanwhile, thinly slice enough of the scallion greens to equal ¼ cup and set aside (discard any remaining greens). Transfer about half of the soup to a blender. Remove the center knob on the blender lid to allow steam to escape, and cover the hole loosely with a towel. Blend until smooth. Return to pot; stir well. Taste and add a bit more salt or pepper if you like. Sprinkle soup with sliced scallion greens; serve immediately. ◇

STARS OF THE NORTH WILD RICE SALAD

Except for the salt and pepper, every ingredient in this salad is produced here in the northland: genuine wild rice, cranberries (did you know that about half of all cranberries sold commercially in the United States are grown in Wisconsin?), hazelnuts (which grow in the wild in much of our area), ramps, apples, sunflower or pumpkin seed oil, and, of course, maple syrup. If you can't get ramps at the farmers' market—or by gathering them yourself in spring—feel free to substitute locally grown green onions; they are almost always available at farmers' markets and co-ops. Cold-pressed virgin sunflower oil is produced in Pierz, Minnesota, by Smude Farms; pumpkin seed oil is produced in Prairie Farm, Wisconsin, by Hay River Foods. (For excellent local vinegar, look for artisanal products from Leatherwood Vinegary in Long Prairie, Minnesota.)

A note about wild rice: I buy only genuine wild-grown rice that has been hand harvested and traditionally finished. Its flavor and texture are far superior to those of the commercial paddy-grown variety, which has been selectively crossbred to make it more disease resistant and easier to harvest; the paddy-grown stuff is also processed differently and lacks the rich, nutty character of truly wild varieties. Occasionally, a news item or other report implies that wild rice has been genetically modified and planted near true

>>

wild rice stands. To date, this scenario does not seem to be reality, although some take it as an ominous sign that the University of Minnesota has done genetic studies on wild rice and also engaged in crossbreeding strains to produce—some say engineer—*a "superior" strain which is, indeed, sometimes planted alarmingly close to stands of native wild rice.*[12]

*Manoomin—*wild rice—*is sacred to the Ojibwe and also has important economic and cultural significance to tribe members. I prefer to support traditional wild rice harvesting rather than encourage the possibility of genetic modification by purchasing paddy-grown rice. Look for genuine wild-grown rice at co-ops, natural-foods stores, and specialty markets; it will always say "hand-harvested and hand-finished" (or words to that effect).*

Note: The method used here for skinning hazelnuts comes from Rose Levy Beranbaum's The Pie and Pastry Bible; *Rose learned it from Cuisinart founder Carl Sontheimer. This technique is way more effective—and less frustrating—than using towels to rub the skins off toasted nuts, which is the method recommended in most cookbooks. Try it and see what you think.* **SERVES 4**

....

1½ cups water

2 tablespoons baking soda

⅓ cup whole, raw hazelnuts (about 1½ ounces)

2½ tablespoons maple syrup, preferably grade B, divided

⅓ cup sunflower or pumpkin seed oil

1½ tablespoons cider vinegar or other vinegar

¼ teaspoon salt, or to taste

⅛ teaspoon freshly ground black pepper, or to taste

2 cups cooked, cooled wild rice (see head note)

⅓ cup dried cranberries

2–3 ramps, bulbs thinly sliced and leaves cut into thin ribbons, or substitute 3 green onions, white and green parts, thinly sliced

½ medium Honeycrisp or other crisp apple, cored, cut into ¼-inch cubes

....

Heat oven to 350 degrees. Line a small, heavyweight rimmed baking sheet with foil; coat foil with cooking spray and set aside. In medium nonaluminum saucepan, heat water to boiling. Stir in baking soda; the water will foam up vigorously. Add hazelnuts. Cook for 3 minutes, watching to ensure it doesn't boil over. Dump the mixture into a wire-mesh strainer and rinse with cold water, then slip the skins off with your fingers. As you skin each nut, press it firmly to separate it into 2 halves. If some nuts won't separate, place them on a work surface and press on them with the flat side of a table knife to separate the halves. Pat all skinned nut halves with paper towels, then spread on the prepared baking sheet. Bake nuts for 5 minutes and remove from oven. Pour 1 tablespoon syrup over the nuts, stirring to coat. Return to oven and bake until the nuts are golden brown, 10 to 12 minutes, stirring twice; don't let them get too brown as they will continue to darken after they are removed from the oven. Remove pan from oven and set aside until nuts are cool.

In a small jar, combine remaining 1½ tablespoons syrup with the oil, vinegar, salt, and pepper. Cover tightly and shake well to blend; taste for seasoning and adjust salt or pepper if needed.

In mixing bowl, combine wild rice, cranberries, sliced ramps, apple cubes, and cooled hazelnuts; toss to mix. Re-shake dressing and drizzle it over the rice mixture, tossing to coat; you probably won't need all of the dressing (leftover dressing will keep, refrigerated, for several weeks). Serve salad immediately or cover and refrigerate for up to 4 hours, bringing to cool room temperature and re-tossing before serving. ◊

Beet, Fennel, and Winter Fruit Salad

I don't know who came up with the idea of pairing beets, fennel, and apple, but it's a brilliant combination. In this salad, the trio is arranged on a bed of spinach; oranges and pomegranate seeds add color and a sweet-tart punch. Serve as a first course or alongside a rich main dish like stew. **SERVES 4**

3 medium beets

½ cup water, plus more as needed

1 teaspoon plus 1 tablespoon maple syrup, divided

3 tablespoons olive oil

1 tablespoon finely chopped shallots

1 tablespoon freshly squeezed lemon juice

2 teaspoons Dijon mustard

¼ teaspoon freshly ground black pepper

1 orange

1 medium bulb fennel

1 apple (Honeycrisp, Braeburn, or Fuji all work well here)

4 cups baby spinach

2 tablespoons pomegranate seeds, optional

1½ tablespoons coarsely chopped fresh dill (do not substitute dried dill)

Peel beets and slice ¼ inch thick, then cut slices into ¼-inch-wide strips. Place in medium skillet; add water and 1 teaspoon syrup. Heat to boiling over medium-high heat, then reduce heat so mixture is boiling gently and cook until beets are tender, 10 to 15 minutes. If all the liquid cooks away, add a little more water, but you want to end up with very little water left when the beets are cooked. Transfer beets and clinging juices to a bowl and set aside to cool. The beets can be prepared a day or two in advance: cover and refrigerate until needed, then remove from refrigerator an hour before you're ready to assemble the salad.

The dressing can also be prepared a day or two in advance. To make the dressing, combine the remaining tablespoon syrup with the oil, shallots, lemon juice, mustard, and pepper in a glass jar. Cover tightly and shake well to blend. Refrigerate until needed, then remove from refrigerator an hour before you're ready to assemble the salad.

Use a sharp paring knife to remove the rind from the orange, cutting generously so that all the white pith is removed. Cut the orange into segments by slipping the knife as close as possible next to the membrane, freeing the segments; discard the membranes, and set the cleaned orange segments aside. Cut the stalks off the fennel; snip off and reserve some of the feathery green fronds, and discard the stalks (or use for another purpose, like making stock). Cut fennel bulb into quarters vertically, then cut out and discard the core. Slice fennel quarters vertically, about ⅛ inch thick; set aside. Quarter and core the unpeeled apple; slice quarters vertically into thin half-moons.

Spread the spinach on a large serving platter. Arrange the fennel on top of the spinach. Distribute the beets over the fennel, then arrange the apple slices over the beets. Use your fingers to break each orange segment into ½-inch pieces, holding each segment over the salad so the juices drip over the apple slices and vegetables and scattering the orange pieces over the vegetables. Shake the dressing well, and drizzle over the salad. Scatter the pomegranate seeds (if using) over the salad; sprinkle with the dill and the fennel fronds. Serve immediately. ◇

Watercress and Grilled Pear Salad with Serrano Ham and Gorgonzola

This salad brings together a wonderful combination of ingredients that complement one another beautifully; no single flavor dominates. Each pear makes two salads, so the other ingredients are also written for two (except the dressing, which makes enough for six servings). This combination makes a fabulous first course or side dish with soup; you can also serve it as a wonderful luncheon, paired with warm biscuits. Note: Use a pear that is still just a bit firm; if it's too soft it will fall apart during grilling. If you have the grill going for something else, use it to cook the pears (it's not worth lighting the grill just for this dish, which requires about five minutes of grill time); otherwise, a ridged stovetop grill pan works just as well. **SERVES 2**

MAPLE-ORANGE DRESSING

- 3 tablespoons sunflower oil or extra-virgin olive oil
- 2 tablespoons maple syrup
- 2 tablespoons freshly squeezed orange juice (from about ½ orange)
- 1 teaspoon very finely minced shallot
- ½ teaspoon (slightly mounded) Dijon mustard

  few grinds black pepper

- 6–8 leaves butter or gem lettuce (red-edged leaves look very nice)
- 1½–2 cups watercress leaves
- 2 very thin slices Serrano ham, or substitute prosciutto
- 1½ teaspoons sunflower oil or extra-virgin olive oil
- 2 teaspoons maple syrup
- 1 firm-ripe red d'Anjou or Starkrimson pear, skin on, quartered, and cored (see head note)
- ⅓–½ cup Gorgonzola crumbles, or substitute blue cheese

Make the maple-orange dressing: Combine dressing ingredients in a half-pint jar. Cover tightly and shake very thoroughly. Set aside at room temperature while you prepare the salads. (Refrigerate the dressing if made more than an hour in advance.)

Prepare the salads: Line two large salad plates with the lettuce, arranging the leaves with the base ends in the center of the plate; you don't have to cover the plate completely with lettuce, but there should be a nice bed, which will take 3 or 4 leaves per plate. Pile a nice handful of watercress on top of the lettuce. Tear the ham into irregularly shaped pieces, each less than an inch across; arrange them over the watercress. Set the plates aside; if prepared more than 15 minutes in advance, cover loosely with plastic wrap and refrigerate until needed.

If you have a hot grill ready, use it to grill the pears; otherwise, heat a stovetop grill pan (see head note). In a small dish, stir together the oil and syrup until well blended. Roll the pear quarters in the syrup mixture, turning to coat; spoon a bit of the mixture over the cut sides to ensure that every spot has been coated. Place pears on the heated grill or grill pan with one of the cut edges down. Cook for 2 minutes or until nicely marked, then turn the quarters so the other cut edge is down and cook for 2 minutes longer. Gently turn the pears so the skin side is down and cook for 2 minutes longer. Transfer to a cutting board and slice the pear quarters crosswise, about ¼ inch thick or a little thicker. Arrange two pear quarters on each salad; you may scatter the pieces if you like or keep the slices for each quarter together, fanning them slightly. Scatter half of the Gorgonzola crumbles over each salad. Shake the dressing again, then drizzle about a tablespoon over each salad; serve immediately. Leftover dressing will keep for a week or longer in the refrigerator. ◊

Red Cabbage and Berry Salad

Ever get a craving for fresh, raw, colorful vegetables and fruits that are simply prepared? Here's the perfect fix. I came up with this combination one day when I was staring down a half of a red cabbage lurking in the crisper drawer. Suddenly I knew I wanted to combine it with blueberries and raspberries. The method just came together as I was fixing supper, and I have to say, it's really delicious. I'm sure it's chock-full of vitamins and antioxidants; deep purple, red, or blue foods simply radiate good health. **SERVES 4–5**

½ medium red cabbage (you might not need it all)

½ cup thinly sliced white onion

2 tablespoons white wine vinegar

1½ teaspoons kosher salt

½–¾ orange, peeled

1 tablespoon maple syrup

2 teaspoons olive oil or vegetable oil
(Smude Farm's sunflower oil is very good here)

1 cup fresh blueberries

½ cup fresh raspberries, large berries halved before measuring

Cut cabbage into two quarters. Remove core from one quarter and discard, then cut the wedge crosswise into ¼-inch-wide slices. You'll need about 3 cups of sliced cabbage, so you may also need to core and slice some of the second quarter. In large nonreactive mixing bowl, combine sliced cabbage, onion, vinegar, and salt; stir well. Set aside at room temperature to marinate for 25 to 30 minutes, stirring several times. At the end of the marinating time, fill the bowl with cold tap water and swirl the cabbage to rinse off the salt and vinegar. Pour into a wire-mesh strainer and drain, then rinse again; let drain for 5 to 10 minutes.

While cabbage is draining, separate the orange into segments. Use your fingers to break each segment into ½-inch pieces, holding the segment over the empty mixing bowl so the juices drip into the bowl; add the orange pieces to the bowl as you go. Add syrup and oil to the bowl; stir to mix. Return drained cabbage mixture to the bowl; add blueberries and raspberries and stir gently to mix. ◇

SALAD FIXINGS: GLAZED PECANS AND MAPLE-DIJON VINAIGRETTE

Here are simple fixings for a great mixed-greens salad; use both together or just one. This combination is particularly good when used on a spinach salad topped with crumbled soft cheese such as goat cheese or blue cheese. Leftover nuts keep for a week or longer at room temperature if stored in a tightly sealed container. They're great for salads later in the week or as a delightful nibble. The dressing will keep for a week or longer in the refrigerator. **MAKES 1 CUP NUTS, ¾ CUP DRESSING**

>>

....

GLAZED PECANS

1 tablespoon butter

1½ tablespoons maple syrup

1 cup pecan halves or coarsely chopped pecans
(3¼–3½ ounces)

MAPLE-DIJON VINAIGRETTE

6½ tablespoons extra-virgin olive oil

2½ tablespoons champagne vinegar
or other mellow white wine vinegar

2 tablespoons maple syrup

1 tablespoon Dijon mustard

....

For the pecans: Heat oven to 400 degrees. Line a rimmed baking sheet with foil; a half-size baking sheet works great for this amount of nuts, but a full-size one is also fine. In small microwave-safe mixing bowl, melt butter in microwave on high, about 1 minute (keep an eye on it; if it cooks too long it will spatter). Add syrup and stir until well mixed. Add nuts, stirring to coat. Scrape onto prepared baking sheet, spreading out in a single layer. Bake until nuts look burnished and are beginning to darken but not burn, stirring several times; total cooking time is about 10 minutes. Remove baking sheet from oven and let nuts cool on baking sheet before using; you may need to break them up a bit.

For the vinaigrette: Combine dressing ingredients in a 1-cup jar. Seal tightly and shake well until emulsified. Store leftovers in refrigerator; shake well before using.

Variations: For an extra flavor hit for the pecans, add ⅛ teaspoon curry powder, chili powder, or five-spice powder at the same time as the maple syrup; another option is a generous pinch of cayenne pepper or chipotle chile powder. ◊

Escarole and Radish Salad with Smoky Maple Dressing

Similar to a wilted lettuce salad, with some significant differences. The dressing is close to room temperature, and escarole is thicker than greens typically used for wilted salads, so it remains crisp. Its slight bitterness pairs well with the sweet dressing that gets a nice smoky flavor from bacon. Radishes add color and a peppery bite. **SERVES 4**

- 3 slices thick-cut bacon
- extra-virgin olive oil, if needed
- 2 tablespoons minced red onion
- 1 clove garlic, minced or pressed
- 1 tablespoon plus 1 teaspoon maple syrup
- 1 tablespoon white wine vinegar
- ½ teaspoon Dijon mustard
- ¼ teaspoon Worcestershire sauce
- 8 cups escarole, torn into large bite-size pieces before measuring (about half of a large head)
- 3 radishes, thinly sliced

In medium skillet, cook bacon over medium heat until crisp. Transfer bacon to paper towel–lined plate and set aside. Measure bacon drippings: if there is more than 2 tablespoons, discard the extra, but if there is less than 2 tablespoons, add extra-virgin olive oil to make up the difference. Return the 2 tablespoons bacon drippings to skillet and place over medium-low heat. Add onion and garlic; cook, stirring constantly, for about 2 minutes. Remove from heat and add the syrup, vinegar, mustard, and Worcestershire sauce; whisk to blend. Set aside to cool while you place the escarole in a large salad bowl. Scatter the radishes over the escarole. Crumble the bacon over the top. Bring the salad to the table. Pour the dressing over the top, then toss well to coat and serve immediately. ◇

GRILLED CAMEMBERT AND PEAR SANDWICH

Use artisan-style bread with a fairly firm texture; the ideal loaf is perhaps four inches across and three inches tall. If you have a panini press, you can prepare this sandwich in it. For an even more delicious sandwich, substitute Délice de Bourgogne or another triple-cream cheese for the Camembert.

PER SANDWICH

- 2 ounces ripe, very soft Camembert or Brie (about 4 [1-inch] cubes; see head note)
- 1 teaspoon maple syrup
- 2 slices whole-grain, sourdough, or Italian bread, each about ½ inch thick
- ¼ perfectly ripe Bosc, Starkrimson, or d'Anjou pear, core removed
- 2 teaspoons unsalted butter, very soft, divided

In small bowl, combine cheese and syrup. Mash with a fork until well combined; the cheese may still be somewhat chunky, but there should be no unabsorbed syrup. Divide the mixture between the two bread slices, spreading evenly on one side of each. Slice the pear lengthwise, about ⅛ inch thick, arranging over the cheese on one slice of bread. Top with second bread slice, cheese-side down, and press together. Spread half of the butter on the top side of the sandwich.

Heat a griddle or heavy skillet over medium heat until hot but not smoking; it should be cooler than it would be for cooking pancakes. Place the sandwich, buttered-side down, on the griddle. Use a metal spatula to press down on the sandwich for about a minute; if cooking more than one sandwich, press one for a minute, then move on to the next one while the first one continues to cook. Spread the remaining butter over the top side of the sandwich, being careful not to burn yourself. Cook the sandwich until golden brown on the bottom, about 4 minutes total including the time spent pressing with the spatula. Carefully turn the sandwich and cook until the second side is golden brown and the cheese is starting to ooze out, 2½ to 3 minutes. Serve immediately with a knife and fork. ◇

TURKEY SANDWICHES WITH
MAPLE-SUNFLOWER CREAM CHEESE

This sweet and crunchy cream cheese spread is easy to make and keeps for several weeks in the fridge. In addition to working well on sandwiches, it is great smeared on a toasted bagel, and it makes a tasty accompaniment to a platter of raw vegetables, cut-up apples, and crackers. **SERVES 4**

MAPLE-SUNFLOWER CREAM CHEESE

1 (3-ounce) package plain cream cheese, softened

2 tablespoons roasted sunflower nuts, salted or unsalted

1 tablespoon maple syrup

4 whole-grain sandwich buns (I like Brownberry's Multi-Grain Sandwich Thins) or 8 pieces sturdy whole-grain bread

1½ teaspoons Dijon mustard, or to taste

8 ounces thinly sliced cooked turkey

romaine or red-leaf lettuce, torn slightly larger than bun size

To prepare the maple-sunflower cream cheese, place cream cheese in a small mixing bowl and mash with a fork. Add sunflower nuts and syrup; stir until well blended. If mixture seems too soft for spreading, refrigerate for a bit until it firms up.

To prepare the sandwiches, spread one-quarter of the maple-sunflower cream cheese on the bottom half of each bun. Spread mustard on the top halves. Top bottom halves with turkey. Place some lettuce on each sandwich, then add the top halves of the buns. Serve immediately or wrap and refrigerate for several hours.

Variation: Cucumber Sandwiches with Maple-Sunflower Cream Cheese

For a vegetarian option, omit turkey; spread buns with cream cheese mixture and mustard as directed. Arrange 6 or 7 thin slices of cucumber per sandwich on each bottom half. Top with a small pile of alfalfa sprouts. Place the lettuce on the sprouts, and add the top halves of the buns. ◈

HIKER'S ENERGY SANDWICHES

I've been enjoying this sandwich since I was a Girl Scout. In this updated version, maple syrup replaces the honey we used to sweeten the mixture back then. These sandwiches travel really well when sturdy bread is used; we often take them along in the backpack when we go hiking, snowshoeing, or canoeing and enjoy the energy boost we get from them at lunchtime. Depending on how you divide the mixture, you'll have enough filling for three hefty sandwiches or four smaller ones. **MAKES 3–4 SANDWICHES**

¼ cup peanut butter (I prefer chunky, but smooth works fine)

1½ tablespoons maple syrup

1 cup shredded carrot, fairly firmly packed
   (about 2 medium carrots)

¼ cup roasted sunflower nuts, salted or unsalted

3–4 whole-wheat pita pocket breads, slit at the top with
     halves loosened but not completely separated

In medium mixing bowl, combine peanut butter and syrup; stir until very thoroughly mixed. Add carrot and sunflower nuts; stir well. Divide mixture between the pita breads. Leftover spread can be refrigerated in a tightly sealed container for up to a week.

Variations:

- Add ¼ teaspoon cinnamon to the peanut butter–maple mixture.
- Substitute almond butter or cashew butter for the peanut butter.
- Substitute bagels, whole-wheat bread, or flat sandwich rounds for the pitas.
- Add 2 to 3 tablespoons dried cranberries or raisins to the mixture.
- Substitute coarsely chopped pecans, walnuts, or almonds for the sunflower nuts.
- Make your sandwiches Elvis-style by spreading some mashed banana on one side of the bread. ◊

Vegetables
and Sides

I t's not hard to imagine carrots or winter squash cooked with butter and maple syrup, similar to the more traditional versions prepared with brown sugar. Root vegetables aren't the only ones that work well with maple, though; in this chapter you'll find a caramelized onion topper paired with asparagus, tangy grilled radicchio brushed with maple, even kale—yes, kale!—parboiled with carrots and tossed with a maple-seasoned dressing. Starchy sides work well with maple, too, as demonstrated by corn on the cob with a spicy maple glaze and a delicious riff on baked beans that features maple and chopped apple.

ROASTED ASPARAGUS AND BELL PEPPERS WITH MAPLE CARAMELIZED ONIONS

These deliciously caramelized onions make a fabulous topper for a colorful blend of asparagus and red bell pepper. The onions work great with other vegetables as well: try roasted cubes of butternut squash, grilled eggplant slices, or steamed broccoli or green beans. **SERVES 4**

2 tablespoons unsalted butter

2 medium white onions (about 1 pound total), sliced vertically into ¼-inch-thick wedges

2½ tablespoons maple syrup

1 pound asparagus spears

1 red bell pepper, cored, sliced vertically into ⅜-inch-wide strips

2 teaspoons olive oil

salt and freshly ground black pepper

finely crumbled Cotija, Parmesan, or feta cheese for garnish, optional

Heat oven to 400 degrees. Melt butter in a heavy-bottomed large skillet over medium heat. Add onions, stirring to coat. Cook, stirring occasionally, until onions are golden and tender crisp, about 10 minutes, reducing heat slightly if onions are getting dark around the edges. Reduce heat to medium-low and stir in syrup. Continue cooking, stirring frequently, until onions are very tender and richly browned, 15 to 20 minutes longer; reduce heat if the onions threaten to burn. Remove from heat and cover to keep warm; set aside until needed.

Break off the hard bottoms of the asparagus, and use a swivel-bladed vegetable peeler to peel the bottom third of each stalk. Place on heavyweight rimmed baking sheet. Add bell pepper strips. Drizzle oil over asparagus and peppers, tossing with tongs to coat. Sprinkle with salt and pepper to taste. Bake, turning occasionally with tongs, until asparagus is tender crisp, 10 to 15 minutes. Transfer vegetables to serving platter. Spoon caramelized onions over the asparagus and bell peppers; top with about ¼ cup crumbled cheese if you like. Serve at once. ◊

GRILLED RADICCHIO WITH MAPLE DRIZZLE AND GOAT CHEESE

Grilling mellows the bitterness characteristic of radicchio, a red-hued member of the endive family. The maple drizzle further sweetens the dish; creamy goat cheese adds wonderful flavor and texture. **SERVES 4**

MAPLE DRIZZLE

- 2 tablespoons extra-virgin olive oil
- 2 tablespoons maple syrup
- 1 tablespoon freshly squeezed orange juice
- ½ teaspoon Dijon mustard
- ¼ teaspoon kosher salt
- ¼ teaspoon freshly ground black pepper
- 1 clove garlic, pressed or finely minced

>>

2 small heads radicchio (about 10 ounces each)

2 teaspoons seasoned rice vinegar

2 tablespoons pine nuts

olive oil as needed (about ¼ cup)

¼ cup crumbled goat cheese (about 1½ ounces)

....

Prepare grill for direct medium-high heat. In small bowl, combine maple drizzle ingredients (on page 79) and stir briskly with a fork; set aside to allow flavors to combine while you prepare the radicchio.

Remove any leaves from the radicchio that look like they're about to fall off (save for use in salads). Cut each head of radicchio lengthwise into 4 wedge-shaped quarters; the cores should hold the radicchio together. Arrange in a single layer, cut sides up, on a plate or glass baking dish. Sprinkle vinegar evenly over the cut sides; set aside to marinate for 5 to 10 minutes. While radicchio is marinating, toast pine nuts over medium heat in a small cast-iron or other heavy skillet until just beginning to brown in spots, stirring frequently; total cooking time will be 2 to 5 minutes. As soon as nuts have started to brown, transfer to a bowl and set aside to cool.

When you're ready to grill, lightly brush radicchio on all sides with oil. Place radicchio on grill grate with a cut side down. Cook until browned, 2 to 3 minutes. Turn the quarters so the other cut side is down and cook for 2 to 3 minutes longer, then turn and cook the outsides of the quarters for 2 to 3 minutes. Transfer to a serving platter with the cut sides up. Drizzle evenly with the maple mixture. Sprinkle goat cheese and toasted pine nuts over the radicchio. Serve immediately or let cool slightly and serve warm. ◇

SWEET AND SOUR CABBAGE

Don't be dismayed if the cabbage looks drab and dreary when it's in the first stage of cooking; the addition of vinegar perks up the color as well as the flavor. This super-easy side dish goes well with grilled chops or steaks; it's also a good accompaniment to roasted poultry. Leftovers make a delicious cold salad. **SERVES 4**

1 teaspoon vegetable oil

1 teaspoon toasted sesame oil
(or a second teaspoon vegetable oil)

¼ medium white onion, sliced crosswise ⅛ inch thick

½ (2-pound) red cabbage, quartered, cored,
and sliced crosswise ½ inch thick

2 tablespoons seasoned rice vinegar

2 tablespoons maple syrup

salt and pepper

3 tablespoons snipped chives for garnish, optional

In large skillet, combine vegetable oil and sesame oil; heat over medium heat until oil is just hot. Add onion; sauté for 3 to 4 minutes, until beginning to color. Add cabbage; cook for 5 minutes longer, stirring several times to separate the cabbage pieces. Add vinegar and syrup, stirring to combine. Cover and reduce heat to low; cook for 5 minutes. Uncover skillet and increase heat to medium; cook for about 5 minutes longer or until cabbage is cooked through and most of the liquid has been absorbed. Taste for seasoning and add salt and pepper as desired; depending on your rice vinegar, the dish may not need any additional salt, but some freshly ground pepper is very good. Sprinkle with chives (if using) before serving. ◇

Maple Baked Beans with Pork Cracklings

Beans baked with maple are often referred to as Canadian or Vermont baked beans—a contrast to Boston baked beans, which are seasoned with molasses. Canada and Vermont are both major producers of maple syrup, so the use of maple is natural. In Canadian maple syrup camps, maple baked beans are often served with eggs and ham—and all are drizzled with additional maple syrup at the table. South of the border, some Vermont cooks regionalize the dish by adding a chopped apple to the pot along with the beans. In my recipe, pork belly replaces the traditional salt pork, which is not only highly salty but typically laden with preservatives. Serve this dish with Sweet Brown Bread with Maple (page 94) for a traditional meal. **SERVES 8–10**

....

1	pound navy beans (also called pea beans)
1	gallon bottled spring water or regular tap water (see note on page 83)
6	ounces pork belly without rind
2	cups diced onion (¼-inch dice)
1	cup chopped Granny Smith or other tart apple
1	cup maple syrup, preferably grade B
2	teaspoons dry mustard
1½	teaspoons salt
½	teaspoon freshly ground black pepper

....

Start the night before you want to bake the beans. Pick through the beans, discarding any stones or weird-looking shriveled-up beans. Rinse the beans, then put them in a large bowl or pot and add spring or tap water (see note on page 83) to cover them by at least 2 inches. Set aside at room temperature until the next day.

When you're ready to cook the beans, drain them. Some cooks save the soaking water to use for cooking the beans, while others use fresh water; the soaking water contains vitamins and minerals, but fresh water (my choice) seems to reduce the flatulence caused by beans. Transfer the drained beans to an enameled Dutch oven or large ceramic bean pot; set aside.

Place pork belly flat on a cutting board, and cut into slices that are just under ¼ inch thick. Cut slices crosswise into ¼-inch-wide strips. Add to a heavy skillet and cook over medium-low heat, stirring occasionally, until crisp and golden brown on all sides. Use a slotted spoon to transfer the browned pork to a paper towel–lined plate; blot with another paper towel and add to the beans, along with the onion and apple. (After the rendered fat has cooled, pour it into a glass jar and store it, tightly covered, in the refrigerator; use it for frying potatoes and the like.)

In measuring cup, stir together the syrup, mustard, salt, and pepper; mix well and add to the beans, stirring to combine. Add enough fresh water or bean soaking liquid to cover the beans by ¼ inch. Cover the casserole and place in the oven. Turn the oven on to 300 degrees. Bake until the beans are just tender but not mushy, 2½ to 3 hours, checking about midway through and adding water if beans are becoming dry; they should always have at least a small amount of water covering them during this stage. Uncover the casserole and bake for 30 minutes longer. Remove from oven and stir the beans; poke most of the pork pieces (which tend to float to the top) down into the beans so only a few are on the surface. Return to oven and bake for 1½ to 2 hours longer; the beans should be moist but not runny and should be somewhat browned on top.

Variations: Substitute 8 ounces thick-cut bacon for the pork belly; reduce added salt to ½ teaspoon. Cut bacon into ½-inch-wide strips and fry it until barely crisp, then proceed as directed. You could also substitute 6 ounces of salt pork, omitting the added salt entirely; cut and fry salt pork as directed for pork belly.

A note about water: Hard water can increase the cooking time of beans, and extremely hard water may even prevent them from softening. I also think that home-softened water may cause problems due to the added salt, to say nothing of softened water's unpleasant taste. Bottled spring water works great for cooking beans, and it's what I use in this recipe. If you choose to use tap water, you may need to adjust cooking times. ◇

CORN ON THE COB WITH SPICED MAPLE GLAZE

This addictive corn can be finished under the broiler or on a grill. For the first step, I prefer to microwave the corn rather than boil it; microwaved corn cooks in its own juices and has a wonderful flavor. Note: If your ears of corn are really large, you may need a somewhat larger pan for the final cooking step. **SERVES 4**

½ cup maple syrup

2 tablespoons unsalted butter

1 clove garlic, pressed or finely minced

½ teaspoon chili powder

pinch salt

few grinds fresh black pepper

4 ears corn, husked

In a heavy-bottomed small saucepan, combine syrup, butter, garlic, chili powder, salt, and pepper. Place over medium heat and cook, stirring several times, until butter melts. Continue cooking until mixture comes to a gentle boil, then cook for 5 minutes or until beginning to thicken, stirring frequently and adjusting heat so mixture continues bubbling but does not boil over. Remove from heat and set aside. (If you prepare the glaze more than 15 minutes in advance, the mixture will begin solidifying into a soft caramel; re-warm it over low heat for a minute or two, stirring several times, until liquefied and smooth.)

If you'll be finishing the corn under the broiler, line an 8- or 9-inch-square pan with heavy-duty foil (see head note); if you'll be finishing the corn on the grill, you'll need a single-use foil pan that holds the corn in a single layer. Trim the tips off the corn ears if necessary so they fit in the pan. Depending on the finishing method you choose—broiling or grilling—

you need to have the broiler heated (with the rack about 5 inches below the heating element) or the grill ready for direct medium-high heat when the corn is done with its preliminary cooking, so plan accordingly.

For the preliminary cooking, sprinkle corn with a little water and wrap each piece individually in waxed paper, twisting ends to seal. Microwave on high, rearranging several times, for 7 to 8 minutes or until just tender, keeping in mind that young corn cooks more quickly than mature corn. (If you prefer, drop corn into a large kettle of boiling water; return to boiling and cook for 5 to 7 minutes, then remove corn from the kettle and set on a rack to drain.)

To finish under the broiler: Arrange the cooked corn (unwrapped, if microwaved) in the foil-lined pan in a single layer. Brush the corn on all sides with the maple glaze, then pour the remaining glaze over the corn. Place under the broiler and cook until the top of the corn is beginning to brown, about a minute, then use tongs to roll each ear a quarter turn. Continue cooking, rolling each ear every minute or so, until corn is richly golden and spotted with brown on all sides; total broiling time is 4 to 7 minutes. Transfer corn to a serving dish and let cool for a few minutes before serving.

To finish on the grill: Unwrap the corn if necessary and have the maple glaze ready before you start. Place the single-use foil pan on the grate, directly over the coals. Arrange the corn in the pan in a single layer. Pour the maple glaze over the corn, then use tongs to roll each ear in the glaze. Grill for about a minute, then use tongs to roll each ear a quarter turn. Continue grilling, rolling each ear every minute or so, for about 8 minutes. Transfer corn to grate, placing ears along the edges of the hot coals rather than directly above the hottest area; carefully remove the empty pan from the grill so it doesn't burn and smoke. Grill corn, turning frequently, until it is richly golden and spotted with brown on all sides, 2 to 5 minutes. If the coals flame up (from the glaze), quickly move corn away from the flames, cover the grill to smother the flame, and wait a minute or so before continuing. When corn is as browned as you prefer, transfer it to a serving dish and let cool for a few minutes before serving. ◊

Roasted Maple-Glazed Carrots

This basic recipe is easy to modify to your taste. For example, you could substitute cut-up butternut or acorn squash for some of the carrots. You could add some onion wedges at the same time as the garlic; if you don't like garlic, you could eliminate it (although it is wonderful—it gets caramelized and a bit toothy, and the bite is mellowed quite a bit by the roasting). Try different herbs, or add some heat with red pepper flakes or ground Szechuan peppercorns, or some sweetness with spices such as ground nutmeg and ginger. Note: Because the ingredient list is so simple, it's super easy to adjust quantities based on how many servings you want. Tailor the size of your baking dish so the carrots fit in a single layer, if possible; if they overlap a bit, just stir them a few extra times during the roasting. **SERVES 4**

....

1½ pounds carrots, peeled

2½ teaspoons olive oil

freshly ground black pepper

2 tablespoons maple syrup, preferably grade B

4–6 cloves garlic, peeled and sliced ⅛ inch thick

¼ teaspoon crumbled dried marjoram
(or other herb of your preference)

coarse sea salt or kosher salt

....

Heat oven to 425 degrees for a glass dish or to 450 degrees for a metal pan. Cut carrots into 1-inch lengths; if any pieces are ½ inch across or thicker, also cut them in half vertically. Place carrots in 13x9–inch baking dish (see head note). Add oil and a few grinds of black pepper, then stir to coat. Bake, uncovered, for 20 minutes, then add syrup and garlic, stirring well. Bake for 10 minutes longer, then stir again and, if using a glass dish, increase temperature to 450 degrees. Bake for 10 minutes longer or until cooked as you like. Sprinkle marjoram and salt to taste over the carrots; stir well and serve. ◊

Pan-Roasted Cauliflower with Bacon

This preparation is simple but surprisingly tasty. Use golden cauliflower for extra color. **SERVES 3–4**

....

½ head cauliflower, trimmed (½–¾ pound after trimming)

3–4 slices thick-cut bacon, cut crosswise into ½-inch pieces

1 tablespoon maple syrup

1 teaspoon unsalted butter

freshly ground black pepper

....

Cut the cauliflower away from the core in large florets, then slice each floret into ½-inch-thick slices; each piece should have at least one flat side. Set aside until needed.

In a heavy-bottomed large skillet, cook bacon over medium heat until browned and crispy, stirring frequently; reduce heat to medium-low as the bacon nears doneness if it looks like it might burn. Use a slotted spoon to transfer bacon to a paper towel–lined dish; set aside. Drain all but 1 tablespoon bacon drippings from skillet.

Add cauliflower slices; stir to coat with the fat, then arrange the pieces so each has a flat side down. Cook without stirring until the bottom side is richly browned, about 5 minutes. Add syrup and butter; stir to loosen the cauliflower, then flip pieces so the browned side is up. Reduce heat to medium-low and continue cooking without stirring until the cauliflower is cooked through and the second side is browned, about 5 minutes longer. Return bacon to skillet and stir to combine; cook for about a minute longer or until bacon is hot. Grind fresh black pepper to taste over the cauliflower. Serve immediately. ◊

KALE WITH CARROTS AND MAPLE DRESSING

This method of cooking kale yields bright-green, tender-crisp leaves. The maple dressing complements the slightly bitter notes of the kale nicely, and the carrots add great color, texture, and nutrition. Serve this dish alongside simply prepared fish or poultry; it would also go well with grilled steak or ribs or a pasta main dish. For a slightly different flavor that works nicely with the kale, use 1 tablespoon olive oil and 1 tablespoon walnut or pumpkin seed oil. **SERVES 4**

1 bunch curly kale

¾ cup julienned carrots (⅛-inch julienne)

2 tablespoons extra-virgin olive oil (see head note)

1 tablespoon maple syrup, preferably grade B

1 tablespoon freshly squeezed lemon juice

salt and freshly ground black pepper

Place the kale in a sinkful of cold water. Remove pieces one at a time, pulling the leaves away from the tough parts of the stalk and tearing the leaves into bite-size pieces; discard the tough stalks. When you are done, you should have about 10 cups of torn kale leaves, packed moderately firmly.

Place a clean tea towel or several layers of paper towels on a large baking sheet; set aside. Heat a large pot of water to a rolling boil over high heat. Add the kale and carrots. Return to boiling and cook for about a minute, then test a kale leaf; it should no longer seem raw but should still be fairly firm. If it seems too firm, continue cooking, checking again in 30 seconds; don't overcook the kale. When the kale is done to your liking, pour kale and carrots into a colander, shaking to remove as much water as possible. Transfer the kale and carrots to the lined baking sheet, spreading them out to help dry the leaves. Blot gently with another towel, then transfer to a serving bowl. Add the oil, then toss with tongs to coat. Add syrup and lemon juice; toss again. Taste and add salt and pepper as needed, gently tossing one more time. Serve immediately. ◊

GRILLED DELICATA SQUASH RINGS WITH MAPLE GLAZE

Unlike other winter squash, delicata squash can be cooked without peeling because their skins are very thin and tender. They're perfect for grilling; a buttery maple glaze gives them a beautiful finish. **SERVES 2–3**

....

2 tablespoons maple syrup

2 teaspoons unsalted butter

1 delicata squash (about ¾ pound), well scrubbed

approximately 2 teaspoons extra-virgin olive oil or other oil

salt (sea salt flakes are particularly good)
    and freshly ground pepper

....

Prepare grill for direct medium heat. In very small 1-cup saucepan, combine syrup and butter. Cook over medium-low heat, stirring constantly, until butter melts, then adjust heat so mixture boils and cook for about a minute, stirring constantly. Remove from heat and keep warm until needed.

Slice unpeeled squash crosswise into ¼-inch-thick rounds. Use a paring knife to cut out the seeds and stringy material in the center (if you have a round cookie cutter or biscuit cutter of the right size, it works really well and looks prettier). Rub a little oil over both sides of each squash ring. Place squash on grill grate over the fire. Cook for 3 minutes, then turn squash and brush the sides that are now facing up with the syrup mixture. Continue cooking for 3 minutes, then turn and brush the other sides with the syrup mixture. Cook for about 2 minutes or until nicely marked and beginning to brown, then turn and cook the other sides for about 2 minutes longer or until squash is tender. Transfer to serving platter; sprinkle with salt and pepper to taste. ◊

Breads

lthough everything in this chapter includes maple, these aren't just breakfast breads. No-knead focaccia gets brushed with maple and sprinkled with sunflower nuts for a different but delicious dinner bread. Maple and freshly ground cardamom are rolled into a rich, eggy dough to create a delightful swirl of flavor. Boston brown bread is updated with maple in an easy-to-bake loaf shape. You'll also find recipes for tender scones and hearty muffins, both enriched with dried fruit; these are great on the breakfast table or as midafternoon snacks.

CRANBERRY-MAPLE SCONES

Over the years I've tried many methods to produce light, tender scones, including using cornstarch, rice flour, or potato flour to replace some of the all-purpose flour. A recipe from Fine Cooking *magazine finally convinced me that a mix of all-purpose flour and cake flour is the way to go; the generous amount of butter doesn't hurt, either. For the best texture, handle the dough as little as possible and pat it out by hand rather than using a rolling pin.* **MAKES 8 SCONES**

- 1 cup all-purpose flour
- 1 cup cake flour
- 2 teaspoons baking powder
- ½ teaspoon baking soda
- ½ cup (1 stick) cold unsalted butter, cut into ½-inch cubes
- ½ cup dried cranberries
- ½ cup chopped pecans (about 2 ounces)
- ½ cup buttermilk
- ⅓ cup maple syrup, preferably grade B
- ½ teaspoon vanilla extract
- 1 tablespoon sugar

>>

Position oven rack in the center of the oven; heat to 375 degrees. Line a baking sheet with parchment; set aside.

Combine all-purpose flour, cake flour, baking powder, and baking soda in food processor; pulse a few times to mix. Add butter; pulse until the mixture resembles coarse sand with a few pea-size lumps, about 10 pulses. Transfer to a mixing bowl. (Alternatively, sift together the all-purpose flour, cake flour, baking powder, and baking soda into a mixing bowl, then cut the butter into the flour mixture with a pastry blender until the mixture resembles coarse sand with a few pea-size lumps.) Stir in the cranberries and pecans. In measuring cup, stir together the buttermilk, syrup, and vanilla. Add to the flour mixture and stir with a wooden spoon just until everything is moistened; the dough will be sticky.

Turn the dough out onto a lightly floured work surface and pat into a circle just under 1 inch thick; pat the edges with your hands until they are even and smooth, then cut into 8 wedges. Use a spatula to transfer the wedges individually to the prepared baking sheet, spacing them several inches apart. Sprinkle the sugar over the wedges. Bake for about 20 minutes or until firm to the touch and lightly golden on the edges and bottoms. Transfer to a rack to cool for at least 20 minutes before serving; serve warm or at room temperature. ◊

No-Knead Oatmeal-Sunflower Focaccia

Although less common than the standard version, sweet focaccia is popular in Italy, particularly in the northwest. My maple-kissed version isn't quite so sweet; in addition to being good at breakfast, it also works well for snacking and as a dinner bread, especially these days when our palates are more accustomed to sweet dinner breads. The basic no-knead concept is based on Jim Lahey's wildly popular (and often adapted) technique, first popularized in the New York Times *by Mark Bittman. Cooked oatmeal gives the bread body and character; a topping of sunflower nuts adds great texture.* **MAKES 1 FOCACCIA**

....

1¾ cups cold water, divided

½ cup old-fashioned rolled oats

¼ teaspoon salt

4 tablespoons maple syrup, divided

2 cups bread flour

1 envelope (2¼ teaspoons) quick-rise yeast

1½ tablespoons sunflower oil, olive oil, or vegetable oil,
    plus more for greasing dish

2½ tablespoons roasted sunflower nuts, salted or unsalted

....

In saucepan, combine 1 cup water with the rolled oats and salt. Heat to boiling over medium-high heat, then reduce heat and simmer for 5 minutes, stirring frequently. Stir 3 tablespoons syrup and the remaining ¾ cup cold water into the oatmeal. Pour into blender; cover and process until the mixture is fairly smooth but not puréed, 5 to 8 seconds. Pour into a large mixing bowl and set aside until mixture cools to 105 degrees.

Add flour and yeast to cooled oatmeal mixture. Stir with a wooden spoon until just combined, about a minute; the mixture will be somewhat sticky and fairly rough looking. Cover with plastic wrap and let rise until the dough triples in size, 2½ to 3¼ hours.

Coat a 13x9–inch baking dish generously with oil. Scrape dough into the dish. Pour the 1½ tablespoons oil into a small bowl. Dip your fingertips in the oil, then press the dough to the edges of the pan, making it an even thickness. Stir the remaining tablespoon syrup into the oil remaining in the bowl, then drizzle over the dough. Scatter the sunflower nuts over the dough, then use your fingertips to press dimples over the entire surface. Cover dish with plastic wrap and set in a warm spot to rise for 45 minutes; near the end of the rising time, heat oven to 400 degrees for a glass dish or 425 degrees for a metal pan. Remove plastic wrap and bake until bread is golden brown and the center reads 200–205 degrees, 25 to 35 minutes. Transfer pan to a wire rack to cool for at least 20 minutes. To serve, cut lengthwise into 3 strips, then crosswise into 5 strips for a total of 15 pieces. The focaccia is best served warm and fresh, although it is good the next day or two. ◇

SWEET BROWN BREAD WITH MAPLE

Boston brown bread is a recipe that dates back to Colonial days. It was traditionally steamed in a pudding mold, similar to English plum pudding (which is a type of bread rather than a soft, custard-like pudding). The version below is prepared in a standard loaf pan, which is easier to come by than a pudding mold; it also uses maple in place of the original recipe's molasses. Brown bread is often served to accompany baked beans; try it with the Maple Baked Beans with Pork Cracklings on page 82 for a nice pairing. Many people enjoy slices of this bread the next day, pan-fried in a little butter and topped with maple syrup; it's also delicious when toasted and slathered with cream cheese. **MAKES 1 LOAF**

....

  1 teaspoon unsalted butter, very soft

½ cup whole-wheat flour

½ cup rye flour

½ cup cornmeal

  1 teaspoon baking soda

¼ teaspoon salt

¼ teaspoon allspice

⅓ cup dried currants

¾ cup buttermilk

½ cup plus 1 tablespoon maple syrup, preferably grade B

....

Heat oven to 325 degrees. Place a kettle or saucepan full of water over high heat; you'll need a quart or two of boiling water when you begin baking the bread. Rub the butter inside a 9x5-inch metal loaf pan; set aside. You'll also need a large, deep baking dish or large pot such as a Dutch oven to hold the loaf pan during baking.

When the water is just starting to boil, prepare the batter. In mixing bowl, stir together the wheat flour, rye flour, cornmeal, baking soda, salt, and allspice. Add currants; stir to separate and to coat with the flour mixture. In small bowl, combine buttermilk and syrup; stir until well blended. Add buttermilk mixture to the dry ingredients; stir until well mixed. Scrape the mixture into the prepared loaf pan. Cover the top of the loaf pan with heavy-duty foil, pressing foil tightly around the top lip of the pan. Place loaf pan in the large dish; add boiling water to come about halfway up the side of the loaf pan. Place dish in oven and bake for 1½ hours, adding boiling water as necessary to keep the level about halfway up the side of the loaf pan. Carefully stick a metal skewer through the foil, wiggling it gently to enlarge the hole slightly and then pushing it into the bread to check doneness; the bread will feel fairly firm, not mushy, when it is done (and if you insert a quick-read thermometer into the bread, it will read 195–205 degrees when done). If it is not quite done, cover the hole with a piece of freezer tape or masking tape and continue cooking; check again in 10 minutes and every 10 minutes thereafter if necessary until the bread is done.

Place the loaf pan on a rack; remove the foil and cool the bread for 30 minutes before removing from pan. This bread can be stored at room temperature for a day or two, but it's so moist that it may mold after that, so it's best kept in the refrigerator after the first day. ◊

HEARTY FRUIT AND NUT MUFFINS

I got this great recipe from a friend, Kathy Johnson, who adapted a recipe she'd gotten from her sister (and from what I understand, her sister had tinkered with the recipe she got from a friend, and so on). Kathy is a vegan who uses no dairy; I've changed her recipe to use buttermilk and butter, but her vegan version is below. **MAKES 12 MUFFINS**

1 cup all-purpose flour

⅓ cup whole-wheat flour

⅓ cup cornmeal

¼ cup old-fashioned rolled oats

¼ cup sugar

2 teaspoons baking powder

¼ teaspoon baking soda

¼ teaspoon salt

1 cup buttermilk

⅓ cup maple syrup, preferably grade B

2 eggs

½ cup (1 stick) unsalted butter, melted and cooled slightly

¾ cup diced mixed fruit and chopped nuts (see page 97)

Position oven rack in middle of oven and heat to 400 degrees. Line 12-cup muffin tin with paper liners; set aside. In large mixing bowl, stir together all-purpose flour, whole-wheat flour, cornmeal, rolled oats, sugar, baking powder, baking soda, and salt; set aside. In a medium mixing bowl, combine buttermilk, syrup, and eggs; whisk to blend. Add butter and whisk very well. Make a well in the center of the flour mixture and dump the buttermilk mixture in all at once; use a wooden spoon to combine, mixing just until dry ingredients are moistened. Add fruit and nut mixture and fold in gently. Spoon mixture into prepared muffin cups; the cups may seem very full, but this batter doesn't rise as much as some others. Bake for 18 to 23 minutes or until the tops are nicely browned and a wooden pick inserted in the center comes out clean.

Mixed Fruit and Nut Suggestions

Really, you can use whatever combination you'd like, as long as the dried fruit is cut into pieces that are about ¼ inch and the nuts are chopped to medium texture. Kathy recommends a mix of dried berries, apricots, apples, and prunes along with chopped walnuts; raisins would be a nice substitution for one of the other fruits, and pecans or slivered almonds would work well in place of the walnuts. (If you like, you can use just one or two kinds of fruit.) I suggest a ratio of about ½ cup dried fruit and ¼ cup chopped nuts, but it's up to you. Don't use more than ¾ cup, total, of the fruit and nut mix.

Variation: Kathy's Vegan Hearty Fruit and Nut Muffins

Eliminate the buttermilk and butter. Stir together 1 cup of unsweetened soy milk and 1 tablespoon white vinegar; let stand for 5 minutes before mixing with other ingredients. Use ½ cup buttery-flavored vegan shortening, melted and cooled slightly, in place of the butter. Proceed as directed. ◈

PULL-APART MAPLE BREAD

This bread is similar to what is usually called "monkey bread"—balls of dough piled up in a Bundt pan, to be pulled apart as eaten. In this recipe, the dough is arranged in a single layer in a flat baking dish, providing more crusty goodness. Not overly sweet, this bread works equally well for breakfast, dinner, or snacking. **SERVES 8–12**

DOUGH

2 tablespoons maple syrup

1 egg

approximately 1½ cups whole or 2 percent milk

2 tablespoons unsalted butter, melted and cooled slightly

3½ cups all-purpose flour, plus additional for shaping dough

½ teaspoon salt

1 envelope (2¼ teaspoons) quick-rise yeast

MAPLE BUTTER

4 tablespoons (½ stick) unsalted butter

3 tablespoons maple syrup

pinch salt

Prepare the dough in a large-capacity bread machine (or prepare it by hand, following the standard procedure for yeast breads): Add syrup and egg to 2-cup measure, then add milk to equal 1⅔ cups; beat with a fork until blended. Add milk mixture and all remaining dough ingredients to bread machine according to instructions for your machine. (Some have special yeast dispensers and require the liquids to be added last, on top of the flour; others require the liquid to be added first so it is at the bottom of the mixing pan, with the yeast on top of the flour.) Run the white dough cycle so the dough is kneaded and proofed; watch the dough in the first few minutes of kneading and add a little more milk (or flour) if the dough appears too dry (or too wet).

When dough cycle is complete (or, if making dough by hand, when it has risen once and been punched down), turn it out onto a floured work surface and knead a few times, then cover loosely with a towel and let it rest while you prepare the maple butter.

To prepare the maple butter, place butter in a heavy-bottomed small stainless steel saucepan and melt over medium heat; the butter will be foamy (a stainless steel saucepan is important for browning the butter; if you use dark cookware, you won't be able to see how brown the butter is getting). Continue cooking, swirling pan occasionally, until the butter is sizzling and bubbling; the foam will dissipate and tiny brown flecks will form in the bottom of the saucepan. Remove from heat as soon as you see the flecks forming, then immediately pour the butter into a clean, cool saucepan or a metal bowl; this step prevents the butter from burning in the residual heat of the saucepan. Stir in the syrup and salt.

Lightly coat a 13x9–inch baking dish with cooking spray. Set a small bowl of flour on your work surface. Use floured fingers to pinch off a piece of dough about the size of a walnut. Shape the dough into a ball by pinching one end together repeatedly, drawing up the sides and pinching together until the ball is smooth and well sealed. Drop the ball into the maple butter and roll it around with a fork, then lift it out and let the excess butter drip off before placing it into the baking dish, pinched-side down. Repeat with remaining dough, arranging in baking dish in a single layer. Reserve remaining maple butter, setting the bowl near the oven or in another warm spot. Cover baking dish loosely with a piece of plastic wrap and set aside for 30 minutes or until the dough balls have expanded to fill the dish; near the end of the rising time, heat oven to 350 degrees for a glass dish or 375 degrees for a metal pan.

When bread has risen, uncover and drizzle remaining maple butter over the top. Bake for 22 to 28 minutes or until nicely browned and cooked through; the rolls in the center of the dish should feel springy, not mushy, when pressed lightly with a fingertip. This bread is best served warm, but leftovers are delicious the next day. ◊

Cardamom-Maple Swirl Bread

Like many spices, cardamom loses its pungency fairly quickly after it's ground. Since the cardamom's kick is an important part of this bread, it's worth it to grind the cardamom just before you need it. Buy whole white cardamom pods at a large supermarket or from Penzeys; you'll need about twenty-five pods for this recipe. Split the pod with your thumbnail and pull out the seeds; use the tip of a knife to pick them out if they are stuck. Grind the seeds as evenly as possible with a mortar and pestle; I usually sift the ground cardamom through a fine wire-mesh strainer to separate out any larger pieces, then grind those some more until they will pass through the strainer. Before beginning, please read "Reducing Maple Syrup" on page 14 and "Testing a Thermometer" on page 16. **MAKES 1 LOAF**

DOUGH

2 tablespoons maple syrup

approximately ⅔ cup buttermilk

2 eggs

3 tablespoons unsalted butter, melted and cooled slightly

2½ cups plus 2 tablespoons bread flour

1½ teaspoons quick-rise yeast

¾ teaspoon salt

CARDAMOM-MAPLE FILLING

⅓ cup maple syrup

3 tablespoons unsalted butter, cut into 3 pieces

1 teaspoon ground cardamom (see head note)

½ teaspoon cinnamon

pinch nutmeg

2 teaspoons half-and-half or whole milk

Prepare the dough in a standard-capacity bread machine (or prepare it by hand, following the standard procedure for yeast breads): Add syrup to 2-cup measure, then add buttermilk to equal ¾ cup. In small bowl, beat eggs with a fork until very well blended but not foamy. Add enough of the beaten egg to the maple mixture to equal 1 cup, then add 2 more tablespoons of the egg to the syrup mixture (you will be using a total of ¼ cup plus 2 tablespoons of the egg in the dough). Cover and refrigerate remaining beaten egg; you'll use it to brush on top of the bread before baking it. Add maple mixture and all remaining dough ingredients to bread machine according to instructions for your machine. (Some have special yeast dispensers and require the liquids to be added last, on top of the flour; others require the liquid to be added first so it is at the bottom of the mixing pan, with the yeast on top of the flour.) Run the white dough cycle so the dough is kneaded and proofed; watch the dough in the first few minutes of kneading and add a little more buttermilk (or flour) if the dough appears too dry (or too wet).

About 45 minutes before the end of the dough cycle (or first rising, if making dough by hand), prepare the cardamom-maple filling: Place syrup in a heavy-bottomed small saucepan. Cook over medium heat without stirring until the surface is covered with foaming bubbles, then adjust heat so mixture continues to bubble but does not boil over and cook without stirring until mixture reaches 24 degrees above boiling on a tested quick-read thermometer (see head note; 236 degrees if your thermometer measures boiling water at 212 degrees); this will probably take 2½ to 3 minutes from the time the mixture starts boiling. Remove from heat and add butter; stir constantly until butter melts and mixture is smooth, about a minute longer. Stir in cardamom, cinnamon, and nutmeg. Set aside to cool, stirring occasionally; the mixture needs to be spreadable—no longer fluid but not hard—when you use it. If it is still looking fluid when you turn the risen bread out to begin working with it, refrigerate the butter mixture for a few minutes to firm it up slightly.

When dough cycle is complete (or, if making dough by hand, when it has risen once and been punched down), turn it out onto a lightly floured work surface and knead a few times. Pat into a rough rectangle about an inch thick, then cover loosely with a towel and let it rest for 10 minutes. Coat a 9x5–inch loaf pan generously with cooking spray; set aside.

Uncover the dough and roll it into a rectangle that is about 8½ by 17 inches. Spread cardamom-maple filling evenly over the dough, keeping about an inch of one short end clear of filling. Starting with the other short edge, roll firmly into a log. Pinch the edge together very well to seal and pat the ends in slightly if necessary so the log is about the same width as the loaf pan. Place dough, seam-side down, in prepared loaf pan. Cover with a clean towel and let rise until roughly doubled in size, 45 to 60 minutes; if you press your fingertip gently into the dough, the dent will spring back just slightly when the dough is properly risen.

Near the end of the rising time, arrange two oven racks in the bottom of the oven and remove any racks above them; place a square of foil in the middle of the bottom rack to catch any drips. Heat to 350 degrees for a glass loaf pan or 375 degrees for a metal loaf pan. When dough is properly risen, add half-and-half to reserved egg and beat with a fork; brush over risen dough, discarding any excess. Place loaf pan in center of oven on top rack, above the foil. Bake until the center of the loaf reads 200–205 degrees on a quick-read thermometer, 30 to 40 minutes; loaf will be richly browned. Place loaf pan on a wire rack and cool for 5 minutes. Loosen edges with a table knife and turn the loaf out onto wire rack; let cool completely before slicing. ◊

main
DISHES

maple's dominant flavor is sweet, but it also has both smoky and woodsy undertones that make it a great partner for pork and rich fish such as salmon. You might also be surprised to learn how well it works with dishes as varied as cabbage rolls, pizza, and pecan-crusted chicken.

BABY BACK RIBS WITH MAPLE GLAZE

I'm a huge fan of slow-smoked ribs, so when some friends served us ribs prepared with this oven-cooked method I was quietly skeptical. Two bites into the meal, I was begging them for the recipe. Its simplicity is amazing: the ribs are pull-off-the-bone tender but still have a wonderful, chewy char on the outside. Our friends used bottled barbecue sauce to finish the ribs on the grill; here, a preliminary marinade provides extra flavor and the ribs are finished with a sweet, tangy maple glaze for an irresistible dish. **SERVES 4**

MARINADE

⅓ cup maple syrup

2 tablespoons paprika, preferably smoked Spanish (sweet, not hot; Penzeys is a good source)

1 tablespoon freshly ground black pepper

1½ teaspoons kosher salt

1½ teaspoons onion powder (not onion salt)

½ teaspoon dried thyme leaves

2 racks baby back ribs (1¾–2¼ pounds per rack)

¾ cup maple syrup

¾ cup apple juice or water

¼ cup tomato paste

¼ cup minced or grated white onion

1 tablespoon Dijon mustard

2 teaspoons chili-garlic sauce (such as Tuong Ot Toi)

....

In a small bowl, stir together all marinade ingredients. Cut each rack of ribs into 4 pieces; place in a large nonreactive baking dish. Pour the marinade over the ribs and rub into both sides, distributing it as evenly as you can. Cover dish with plastic wrap and refrigerate at least 4 hours or as long as 8 hours.

For the preliminary cooking, heat oven to 350 degrees. Add about an inch of water to a roaster or other large baking dish. Place a rack in the roaster, propping it up on balls of foil if necessary to raise it above the water. Stack the ribs on the rack; pour any liquid that has accumulated under the ribs into the roaster. Seal the roaster tightly and bake for 1½ hours. Remove roaster from oven and set the lid slightly ajar; let the ribs rest for 30 to 40 minutes. While the ribs are resting, prepare the glaze. Combine syrup, apple juice, tomato paste, onion, mustard, and chili-garlic sauce in a small nonreactive saucepan. Heat to boiling, adjust heat so mixture boils gently, and cook, stirring occasionally, for about 20 minutes.

Once the ribs have rested and the glaze is ready, you can proceed directly to grilling or refrigerate the ribs, loosely covered, for up to 12 hours before grilling; also cool and refrigerate the glaze if you are going to wait more than an hour before grilling the ribs.

When you're ready to grill, prepare a charcoal or gas grill with a direct, medium-intensity fire. Place the ribs on the grate and cook until hot, turning frequently. Brush a generous layer of glaze on the top side of the ribs. Cook for about 2 minutes, then turn ribs over and brush again with glaze. Continue cooking the ribs, turning every few minutes and brushing with additional glaze, until the ribs are crusty and browned in spots, 5 to 10 minutes. Serve with plenty of napkins. ◇

PULLED PORK

Classic southern-style pulled pork is usually prepared by rubbing a pork shoulder roast with spices and slow-smoking it until it can be pulled apart into shreds. This version uses a low-temperature oven instead, making it a good choice for inclement weather. Wood chips are scattered in the bottom of the baking pan—a technique I learned from food author Mark Bittman—giving the pork a wonderful, woodsy flavor without any smoke. (Note: Although there is no smoke, the woodsy scent will fill your kitchen.)

SERVES 8–12

RUB MIXTURE

⅓ cup maple syrup, preferably grade B

2 tablespoons smoked Spanish paprika (sweet, not hot; Penzeys is a good source)

2 teaspoons kosher salt

1 teaspoon dry mustard

½ teaspoon cumin

½ teaspoon freshly ground black pepper

2 cloves garlic, minced or pressed

1 (3- to 4-pound) bone-in pork butt

2 cups applewood or other wood chips suitable for smoking (½–1 inch in size)

1 (8-ounce) can tomato sauce

1½ cups apple juice

½ cup cider vinegar

⅓ cup maple syrup, preferably grade B

sturdy sandwich buns and coleslaw for serving

Combine all rub ingredients in a small bowl; mix well. Rub half of the mixture (about 2½ tablespoons) all over the pork roast. Place pork in a nonreactive baking dish and cover with plastic wrap; refrigerate at least 4 hours or as long as 24 hours. Refrigerate remaining rub mixture.

When you're ready to cook, place oven rack in the lowest position and heat oven to 300 degrees. Place wood chips in the bottom of a large roaster or sturdy baking dish large enough to hold a roasting rack comfortably. Add enough water to moisten the chips without covering them; there should be a bit of water in the bottom of the pan, but the chips should not be submerged. Place a roasting rack on top of the chips, and place the pork on the rack (prop up the corners of the rack with balls of foil if necessary to keep the pork raised above the water). Cover the roaster tightly and wrap a large sheet of foil around the top, sealing the edges; if using a large pan instead of a roaster, use heavy-duty foil to form a slightly elevated tent over the roast, then use additional foil if necessary to cover the top of the pan, sealing it well along the edges. (With either type of pan, the idea is to make a sealed chamber that will allow the wood-scented steam to circulate around the roast without escaping.) Bake for 6 hours without disturbing the pan or foil.

While the pork is roasting, prepare the sauce. In nonreactive saucepan, combine tomato sauce, apple juice, vinegar, syrup, and the remaining rub mixture. Heat to boiling over medium-high heat, then adjust heat so mixture boils gently; cook, stirring occasionally, for about 45 minutes or until somewhat thickened. Cool sauce and refrigerate until needed.

When pork has cooked for 6 hours, unwrap the pan and transfer the pork to a baking dish or deep platter; let cool slightly. While the meat is cooling, divide the prepared sauce into two portions, placing about ¾ cup in a saucepan and the rest in a serving bowl. Warm the portion in the saucepan over medium-low heat.

Pull the pork away from the bones, discarding bones, fat, and any gristle you encounter. Use two forks (or your fingers, if the pork is cool enough to handle) to pull the meat apart into shreds. Combine shredded pork with the warmed sauce in a large serving dish. Serve with the remaining sauce. Traditionally, the meat is piled into a bun, then topped with coleslaw and additional sauce, although some people prefer the coleslaw on the side. ◊

Pork Tenderloin with
Rhubarb-Maple Sauce and Cheese Grits

I came up with this recipe after reading Kim Ode's delightful Rhubarb Renaissance. *She does so many wonderful things with rhubarb that it got me to thinking about ways to combine it with maple. The recipe here is the result. The pan sauce came together almost by itself, and the grits are a great accompaniment. Note: For the timing to work as written, buy a pork tenderloin that is about 1½ inches thick and 2½ inches wide at the largest part. If the tenderloin you use is smaller, the oven cooking time will need to be shortened, so be prepared to check the internal temperature at 15 to 20 minutes. I don't recommend tenderloins that are injected with a seasoned solution; they are typically labeled as "enhanced" or have some sort of claim to extra juiciness. I'd rather control the seasoning myself, plus I don't want to pay pork prices for the weight of the injected solution.* **SERVES 3–4**

1¾ cups chicken broth

1 tablespoon unsalted butter

½ cup stone-ground grits (not instant)

1 whole pork tenderloin (about 1¼ pounds; see head note), trimmed and cut into 2 pieces

salt and freshly ground black pepper

4 teaspoons all-purpose flour

1½ tablespoons vegetable oil

1½ tablespoons plus ½ cup maple syrup, divided

1½ tablespoons Dijon mustard

1½ cups rhubarb, cut into ½-inch pieces

½ cup chopped onion

1 tablespoon rice vinegar

½ teaspoon dried thyme

¼ teaspoon hot pepper sauce

½   cup whole milk

¼   cup freshly grated Parmesan cheese

¼   cup grated Cheddar cheese

....

In a heavy-bottomed large saucepan, combine broth and butter. Heat to boiling over medium-high heat. Add grits in a slow but steady stream, stirring constantly. Return to boiling, then cover and reduce heat to very low and cook for 30 minutes, stirring frequently. Remove from heat and set aside.

While grits are cooking, heat oven to 350 degrees. Season the tops of the pork with salt and pepper to taste, then sprinkle half of the flour over the pork and rub in with your fingertips; turn and repeat. Heat oil in medium skillet over medium-high heat until shimmering. Shake excess flour from pork, then add to skillet and brown on both sides, 6 to 8 minutes total. Transfer pork to a baking dish. In small bowl, stir together 1½ tablespoons syrup and the mustard; brush over both sides of pork. Bake, uncovered, for 30 minutes (set a timer so you don't lose track of the pork).

As soon as the pork goes into the oven, pour off all but 2 teaspoons of the drippings from the skillet and place skillet over medium heat. Add rhubarb and onion; cook over medium heat, stirring occasionally, until rhubarb has softened, 4 to 5 minutes. Add vinegar, thyme, hot pepper sauce, and remaining ½ cup syrup. Adjust heat so mixture bubbles very gently and cook, stirring occasionally, until mixture is saucelike, 4 to 8 minutes longer. Remove from heat and cover to keep warm.

When the pork has cooked for 30 minutes, check the temperature at the thickest area; remove from oven when the center reaches 155 degrees. Cover loosely with foil and set aside.

Stir the milk into the grits and place over medium heat. Cook for 5 minutes, stirring occasionally, then add Parmesan and Cheddar cheeses. Cook, stirring frequently, until cheese melts, about a minute longer.

Slice the pork into 1-inch pieces and arrange on a platter. Serve with rhubarb sauce and grits. ◇

Pecan-Crusted Chicken with Maple Apples

Maple-sweetened apples make a wonderful accompaniment to the crusty, nutty chicken in this easy skillet dish. **SERVES 4**

- 4 (5-ounce) boneless, skinless chicken breast halves
- 1 tablespoon plus ¼ cup maple syrup, divided
- 2 tablespoons Dijon mustard
- ¾ cup chopped pecans (about 2½ ounces)
- ½ cup bread crumbs
- 2 tablespoons unsalted butter
- 1 tablespoon vegetable oil, plus a little more if needed
- 3 large apples (about 1½ pounds total), unpeeled, each cored and cut into 16 wedges
- ½ large onion, cut into ¼-inch-wide wedges
- ¼ cup dry sherry, dry white wine, or chicken broth

Heat oven to 375 degrees. Pound chicken breasts so each is no thicker than ¾ inch. In small bowl, stir together 1 tablespoon syrup and the mustard; brush over both sides of chicken and set aside.

Chop pecans medium-fine in food processor; the texture should resemble uncooked quinoa. In 11x7–inch baking dish, stir together chopped pecans and bread crumbs, mixing well. Coat chicken breasts on both sides with pecan mixture, pressing gently to help nuts and crumbs stick; transfer to a clean plate or piece of waxed paper.

In large skillet, melt butter in oil over medium heat. When butter is foamy, add chicken breasts in a single layer. Cook for 3 to 4 minutes on each side or until the pecan mixture is nicely browned and set. While chicken is cooking, rinse out and dry the baking dish, discarding any remaining pecan mixture. Transfer browned chicken to clean baking dish and bake for 20 minutes; set a timer so you don't lose track of the chicken.

As soon as the chicken is in the oven, begin preparation of the apples. If there are bits of pecan remaining in the skillet that are overly browned, scoop them out and add a little more oil. Add apples and onion to the drippings remaining in the skillet. Cook over medium heat, stirring frequently, for 5 to 10 minutes or until apples are golden brown and beginning to soften. Add sherry, wine, or broth and cook for about 2 minutes, stirring several times. Add remaining ¼ cup syrup. Cook, stirring occasionally, until apples are tender and onions are caramelized, about 5 minutes longer. Check the chicken during this time, and when it is 165 degrees at the thickest part, remove from oven and cover loosely with foil. Arrange the chicken on a serving platter, and spoon the maple apples over the chicken; serve immediately. ◇

STEELHEAD WITH TWO-MUSTARD GLAZE

I love the pop of whole mustard seeds, which pair very nicely with Dijon mustard and maple in this simple glaze; tarragon adds a subtle but delightful touch. This recipe is easy and quick enough for a weeknight but fancy enough to serve to guests. Saffron rice and a bright green vegetable are pleasant accompaniments. **SERVES 4**

1½ pounds boneless, skin-on steelhead fillets, in 4 pieces

2 tablespoons maple syrup

1 tablespoon Dijon mustard

1 teaspoon mustard seeds

1 teaspoon finely minced shallots

1 teaspoon chopped fresh tarragon
or ½ teaspoon crumbled dried

⅛ teaspoon white pepper

Arrange oven rack in upper third of oven; heat to 400 degrees. Line a baking sheet with foil. Place steelhead on baking sheet, skin-side down; pat dry with paper towels. In small bowl, stir together remaining ingredients; spoon and spread evenly over steelhead. Bake for 10 minutes, then turn on broiler and continue cooking until topping is bubbly and browned in spots and steelhead is cooked through, 3 to 5 minutes longer. ◇

Salmon with Maple, Orange, and Herb Glaze à la Birch Lake

This dish was born at a cabin on the Gunflint Trail, where we were staying with friends. They had some Alaskan salmon in the freezer, and one night we decided to grill it. Deb and I concocted the glaze in the kitchen using ingredients that were on hand, while Oscar manned the grill outside. Shortly before the fish was done, we brushed a liberal amount of the glaze on the salmon, then drizzled the rest over the top after it was put on the serving platter. This simple recipe highlights the versatility of maple syrup when it's cooked and tempered with butter. You could substitute other herbs, add mustard, use a liquor such as bourbon in place of the orange juice—I think you get the idea. (Deb and Oscar report that this glaze is also excellent with grilled duck breast.) **SERVES 4**

1½ pounds boneless, skin-on salmon fillets (¾–1 inch thick)

salt

1 navel orange, well scrubbed

⅓ cup maple syrup

¼ teaspoon dried rosemary

¼ teaspoon dried marjoram

few grinds black pepper

1 tablespoon butter

Prepare grill for direct medium heat. Tear off a piece of heavy-duty foil that is just large enough to hold the salmon in a single layer. Sprinkle the salmon lightly with salt and let stand at room temperature while you prepare the glaze.

To prepare the glaze, cut 3 strips of zest, each about ½ inch wide and 1½ inches long, off the orange. In a heavy-bottomed small saucepan, combine syrup with the zest, rosemary, marjoram, and pepper. Heat to boiling over medium-high heat, then adjust heat so the syrup foams and boils steadily without boiling over and cook, stirring constantly, for 5 minutes. Remove from heat and add butter; stir until butter melts. Cut off a chunk of the orange and squeeze the juice into the pan, using your fingers to strain out any seeds; use as much of the orange as needed to get about 2 tablespoons of juice. Pull the zest out of the syrup mixture and set aside for garnish or discard (see note below). The glaze is now ready to use.

Ideally, Oscar (or someone else) will be outside cooking the salmon while you're working on the glaze, but if not, set the glaze aside until it's needed. To cook the salmon, place the foil on the grate, then arrange the salmon, skin-side down, in a single layer. Cover the grill and cook the salmon for 7 to 10 minutes, depending on thickness. Brush some of the glaze (re-warmed if necessary) over the salmon; re-cover the grill and cook for 4 to 5 minutes longer or until done to your preference. To serve, slip a thin-bladed metal spatula between the salmon flesh and the skin, shimmying the spatula under the flesh to gently separate it from the skin; transfer the skinned salmon to a serving platter. Drizzle the remaining glaze over the salmon, and garnish with thinly sliced orange zest if using; serve promptly.

Note: Deb and I discovered that the orange zest, which is candied by the cooking process, makes a pretty good nibble if you like a strong orange flavor; once it had cooled, we gobbled it up while we were hanging around the stove. In subsequent tests of this recipe, I decided to use the zest, sliced very thinly into strips, as a garnish on the cooked fish; if you enjoy candied orange zest, give it a try. Otherwise, simply discard the zest. ◊

Planked Steelhead or Salmon

Cooking on cedar planks is a method usually attributed to the Pacific North-west Indian tribes. For this technique, fish, poultry, or game is placed on thin, flat, soaked cedar planks, which are then put over a bed of coals; the indirect heat keeps the food from drying out (even if it's cooked a bit too long), and the smoldering plank contributes a wonderful woodsy flavor. Planks are available at gourmet supermarkets and sporting-goods stores, and they're not just cedar anymore: maple and other species are available, and each imparts its own unique flavor. Use whatever appeals to you (or, more likely, whatever you can find); make sure the plank is large enough to hold the fish but not too large for your grill. For additional fish portions, use a second plank. Note: Salmon steaks would also work well in this recipe. **SERVES 4**

maple, cedar, or other grilling plank about ½ inch thick

¼ cup maple syrup

2 teaspoons unsalted butter

1 teaspoon lemon juice

½ teaspoon prepared horseradish

2 cloves garlic, minced or pressed

1 quart cold water

¼ cup packed brown sugar

¼ cup kosher salt

4 (5- to 6-ounce) center-cut boneless steelhead or salmon fillets (skin on or skinless)

Soak the plank in a clean bucket filled with cold water for 4 hours, weighting to keep it submerged.

When you're ready to start preparation of the fish, combine syrup, butter, lemon juice, horseradish, and garlic in a heavy-bottomed small saucepan. Heat to boiling over medium-high heat, then cook, stirring almost constantly, for 2 to 3 minutes or until somewhat thickened. Remove from heat and set aside.

Prepare the brine: In large nonreactive bowl, combine water, brown sugar, and salt, stirring until sugar and salt dissolve. Place salmon in a zipper-style gallon food storage bag, then place the bag in a baking dish that holds it comfortably. Pour brine into bag, using enough to cover fish completely; seal bag, pressing out as much air as possible. Refrigerate for 25 to 30 minutes (no longer: if the grill is not yet ready after 30 minutes of brining, drain and rinse the fish and pat it dry, then refrigerate until the grill is ready). While fish is brining, prepare grill for direct high heat. Remove fish from brine, then rinse and pat dry; discard brine.

Place fish on soaked board, skin-side down; if there is a thinner edge portion, fold it under so it doesn't dry out (if you're cooking steaks, simply place them on the board with one cut side down). Brush cooled maple mixture over fish, re-warming slightly if necessary to loosen it up. Place the plank on the grill cooking grate over the hot coals. Cover grill and cook until fish is just beginning to turn opaque in the thickest area, 15 to 20 minutes (if the plank catches fire around the edges, don't worry about it; if the fire looks like it is getting too strong, however, spray the edges with water, avoiding the fish). Serve fish directly from plank or transfer to a serving platter. Discard plank. ✧

PIZZA WITH BRIE, CARAMELIZED ONIONS, BASIL, AND MAPLE

This pizza is a nice change of pace from the usual tomato-topped pies. Serve it with a big salad for a light supper, accompanied by a glass of crisp, fruity red wine or chilled white wine. Preparation for the crust starts a few hours before dinner is served, so plan accordingly. Note: A large pizza peel is the best tool for transferring the pizza to the baking stone. If you don't have one, use a baking sheet that is rimless on one edge or a rimmed baking sheet that has been flipped upside down. **MAKES 1 (10-INCH) PIZZA, TO SERVE 2–4**

CRUST

- 1¼ cups bread flour
- ¾ teaspoon quick-rise yeast
- ½ teaspoon salt
- ½ cup cold water, plus more as needed
- 2 teaspoons extra-virgin olive oil

- 1 tablespoon plus 1 teaspoon extra-virgin olive oil, divided
- 1 large yellow onion, sliced vertically into ¼-inch-thick wedges
- ½ teaspoon crushed red pepper flakes
- 1½ tablespoons maple syrup
- 2 cloves garlic, minced or pressed
- 1 (8-ounce) wheel Brie, sliced into two half-rounds
- freshly ground black pepper
- 15 fresh basil leaves, rinsed and patted dry

To prepare the crust, in food processor, combine flour, yeast, and salt; pulse a few times to mix. Measure ½ cup cold water, then add the oil to the water. With processor running, pour water mixture slowly into feed tube. Let processor run until a cohesive dough is formed; if it looks crumbly and doesn't come together, dribble a little more water into the feed tube. When the mixture has pulled together, let the processor run for 90 seconds. Lightly oil a mixing bowl, then transfer the dough to it, turning to coat. Cover with a clean towel and let rise until doubled in size, about 2 hours.

Near the end of rising time, place a pizza stone on the lower oven rack; heat oven to 500 degrees. (The pizza stone should heat for at least 30 minutes, so be sure to start it early enough. Longer heating won't hurt the stone; it's better to heat it for a longer period than not to have it hot enough.) Heat a tablespoon of the oil in a large skillet over medium heat until warm, then add onion and pepper flakes. Cook, stirring frequently, until onions are golden and tender crisp, about 10 minutes; if onions are getting dark around the edges, reduce heat slightly. Add syrup and garlic. Reduce heat to medium low and continue cooking, stirring frequently, until onions are very tender and richly browned, 10 to 15 minutes longer; reduce the heat if the onions are burning. Remove from heat and set aside until needed.

When the dough is fully risen, turn it out onto a lightly floured work surface; knead several times, then flatten dough with your hands into a 6-inch disk. Set a piece of parchment on a pizza peel (see head note), and transfer the flattened dough to the parchment. With lightly floured fingertips, press the dough into a circle about 10 inches across, keeping the edge a bit thicker (if the dough springs back repeatedly while you are trying to shape it, cover it with a towel and let it rest for 15 minutes before proceeding). Brush the remaining teaspoon of oil over the crust. Prick the dough lightly at 1-inch intervals with a fork.

Slice the Brie across the short direction into ⅛-inch-thick rectangles; arrange over the dough as you go, placing the slices about ¼ inch apart and keeping the cheese away from the edges (you probably won't need the entire 8-ounce wheel). Scatter the browned onions over the cheese, rewarming them slightly if they stick to the skillet. Grind black pepper to taste over the onions. Trim the parchment so it is no more than 2 inches wider than the dough circle (thus preventing an edge of the parchment from contacting the wall of the oven and possibly igniting during baking; trust me on this one). Open the oven and quickly slide the pizza (still on its parchment) off the peel on to the center of the heated stone.

>>

Immediately reduce oven temperature to 475 degrees. Bake for 10 to 12 minutes or until the crust is done in the center and the edges are nicely browned; the cheese should be melted and bubbly. While pizza is baking, stack 5 of the basil leaves and roll into a tight cylinder, rolling parallel with the leaf rib. Slice the cylinder crosswise at ⅛-inch intervals; when they unroll, you will have thin strips of basil (this is called a *chiffonade*). Slice remaining basil in a similar fashion, then fluff the pile of strips to loosen them.

When the pizza is done, remove it from the oven by sliding the parchment back onto the peel, using tongs or a spatula to pull or guide the parchment. Immediately scatter the basil strips over the pizza. Let stand for a minute or two before serving. ◇

FINNISH-STYLE CABBAGE ROLLS

Finnish cabbage rolls have a sweet sauce rather than the tomato-based sauce common to most other cabbage roll recipes; they also typically include barley in the filling rather than the traditional rice. Here I've substituted maple syrup for the molasses that is typically used. These delicious cabbage rolls are great served with lingonberry preserves and mashed or boiled potatoes; fingerling potatoes would be very nice if you go with the boiled option. SERVES 4–6

- 1 large head green cabbage, cored
- ½ pound ground beef
- ½ pound ground pork
- 1 tablespoon chopped fresh marjoram leaves or 1½ teaspoons dried
- ½ teaspoon white pepper
- ½ teaspoon allspice
- ½ teaspoon salt

1 cup cooked barley, cooled to room temperature or chilled

2 tablespoons heavy cream

½ cup plus 3 tablespoons maple syrup, divided

approximately 2 cups low-sodium chicken broth

2 tablespoons unsalted butter

....

Coat a 13x9–inch baking dish with cooking spray; set aside. Heat a large pot of salted water (in the ratio of 1 teaspoon salt to 1 gallon water) to boiling. Slip the cabbage into the water. Begin turning the cabbage over frequently with a large slotted spoon; the outer leaves will release from the core as you turn it. Cook until the loose leaves become pliable and brighter in color, then transfer them to a large bowl. Continue cooking and turning the cabbage; the outer leaves should continue to release so you can remove them as they become tender. Keep going until you have 12 good-size, intact leaves; as you get closer to the core, you may have to use tongs and your spoon to tease the leaves away from the core and might even need to nick the base of the leaf slightly with a long, thin knife if it isn't cut completely through. Remove the rest of the cabbage from the pot and pull off a few of the smaller leaves (or use leaves you've torn accidentally). Chop the extra leaves finely in a food processor; you should have about ¾ cup. Cool, wrap, and refrigerate remaining cabbage for another use.

Begin heating oven to 350 degrees. Add beef, pork, marjoram, pepper, allspice, and salt to food processor with cabbage. Pulse several times to combine; the meat should be chopped a little finer than it was, but don't overprocess and turn it to paste. Scrape the meat mixture into a mixing bowl; stir in barley, cream, and 1 tablespoon syrup. Pick up one cabbage leaf and use a paring knife to shave off the thickest part of the rib, being careful not to cut all the way through. Scoop up about ¼ cup of the meat mixture and pat it into a log about 3 inches long, then place it at the base of the cabbage leaf. Fold the base over the filling and roll it once, then fold in the sides and roll up firmly. Place, seam-side down, in prepared baking dish. Repeat with remaining ingredients. Pour enough chicken broth into the dish to come not quite halfway up the sides of the rolls (you might not use it all); set pan aside.

>>

In a heavy-bottomed small saucepan, heat ½ cup syrup over medium heat until boiling, then adjust heat so syrup bubbles but does not boil over and cook, stirring constantly, for 4 minutes. Remove from heat; add the butter and stir constantly until the butter melts. Drizzle the maple mixture evenly over the cabbage rolls. Cover dish with foil and bake for 45 minutes.

Remove the dish from the oven and uncover. Drizzle remaining 2 tablespoons syrup evenly over the tops of the cabbage rolls. Return uncovered dish to oven and bake for 45 minutes longer. The top of the rolls should be nicely browned when the rolls are done.

Variation: This isn't traditional, but I like to use the liquid remaining in the dish to make a gravy, which is deliciously sweet and goes well with the potatoes. To prepare the gravy, use a slotted spoon to transfer the cooked cabbage rolls to a serving platter; set aside and keep warm. Using a heatproof measuring cup, measure 1½ cups of the liquid remaining in the baking dish, adding more chicken broth as needed. In saucepan, melt 3 tablespoons butter over medium heat. Whisking constantly, sprinkle 3 tablespoons all-purpose flour over the butter. Cook, whisking constantly, until the mixture is golden and smells nutty, 3 to 4 minutes. Whisking constantly, add the measured cooking liquid; cook, whisking frequently, until thickened, about 3 minutes. ◊

Beverages

ever thought about adding a shot of maple syrup to cappuccino, or using it in hot drinks such as whiskey toddies or mulled apple cider? You'll find those ideas here, including an additional surprise: bacon-infused bourbon with maple. There are kid-friendly beverages too: a delicious brown cow float with maple and a creamy maple malt.

MULLED APPLE-MAPLE CIDER

Why is it called mulled, I wonder? I've never known. Anyway, try this pleasant warmer on a cool fall evening or in the dead of winter gathered 'round the fire. The maple syrup adds a subtle, almost smoky taste. **SERVES 4**

1 quart apple cider

¼ cup maple syrup

½ orange, cut into 2 pieces

6 whole cloves

3 whole allspice berries, or dash ground allspice

1 cinnamon stick, plus additional for serving if you like

Combine all ingredients in medium nonaluminum saucepan. Heat over medium heat until simmering, then reduce heat so mixture is steaming (barely simmering) and cook for about 15 minutes. Remove from heat and let stand 5 minutes. Strain into individual mugs through a fine mesh strainer. Slip a whole cinnamon stick into each mug if you like, and serve.

Variation: High-Octane Mulled Cider

Add 2 to 3 tablespoons brandy, bourbon, or rum to each serving. ◇

Brown Cow with Root Beer and Maple

This soda-fountain classic can be prepared in a number of ways. I find that muddling a shot of chocolate syrup and a glug of maple with a small amount of root beer, then adding two layers of ice cream and more root beer, makes a creamy, dreamy treat. **PER SERVING**

1½ tablespoons maple syrup

2 teaspoons chocolate sundae syrup

½ (16-ounce) bottle chilled top-quality root beer
(I prefer Sprecher's, made in Glendale, Wisconsin)

2 scoops vanilla ice cream

Add maple and chocolate syrups to a tall, chilled pint glass. Add about ⅓ cup root beer; stir well with a long-handled spoon. Add a scoop of ice cream and another ⅓ cup root beer; stir slightly. Add another scoop of ice cream; fill glass with root beer and serve immediately with the long-handled spoon and a straw. ◊

Bacon-Infused Bourbon with Maple

I'm not sure who came up with the concept of bacon-infused bourbon; the basic idea has been published in sources as varied as Southern Living *magazine and a number of food blogs including bacontoday.com (no kidding). The smoky taste of bourbon is a natural with bacon, though, and together they pair really well with maple syrup. This infused, sweetened bourbon can be used in any cocktail recipe that calls for bourbon and sugar, such as the Old Fashioned below; it's also delicious straight up or on the rocks. My version makes a smaller amount than other sources: if you like it, you can always make more, and if you don't, well, you haven't wasted too much of anything. Note: You need to infuse the bourbon for a full day before serving it, so plan accordingly before your next snowshoeing party.* **MAKES ABOUT 2 CUPS**

½ pound smoky bacon (I prefer Nueske's Applewood Smoked Bacon, made in Wittenberg, Wisconsin)

1 (375 ml) bottle (about 1⅔ cups) Jim Beam or other bourbon

⅓ cup maple syrup, preferably grade B

Fry the bacon over medium heat until crisp. Transfer bacon to paper towel–lined plate and set aside for other uses. Pour bourbon into a clean pint jar, then add 3 to 4 tablespoons of the still-hot bacon drippings to the jar; discard remaining drippings or reserve for another use. Cover jar and shake well, then let stand at room temperature for 4 hours, shaking occasionally. Place jar in freezer for 24 hours, then strain bourbon through a paper coffee filter set in a small strainer on top of a large measuring cup; you'll have to push the layer of fat aside to pour out the bourbon, but the fat will remain in the jar. (The straining goes pretty slowly; it's best to pour a small batch—maybe ½ cup—into the filter and let that drain, then gently squeeze out the filter to extract any bourbon in the paper and start with a fresh filter.) Stir the syrup into the strained bourbon, then pour into a clean bottle and store in the refrigerator until used.

Old Fashioned with Bacon and Maple

For each cocktail, add ¼ cup infused bourbon and 2 or 3 dashes of bitters to a cocktail shaker filled with ice. Shake and strain into a lowball glass; garnish with a maraschino cherry and an orange slice. Consume (or serve) immediately. Call a cab. ◇

MEYER TODDY

This combo was served to me by some friends when we were staying at their cabin one winter and I came down with a nasty cold. Sure made me sleep good! **PER SERVING**

....

1 shot (3 tablespoons) Early Times or other Kentucky whiskey

1½ tablespoons maple syrup

dash cinnamon or nutmeg

boiling water

1 small pat butter (about ½ teaspoon; salted or unsalted), optional

1 lemon wedge

....

Add whiskey and syrup to an 8-ounce mug. Sprinkle cinnamon or nutmeg into mug and stir briefly. Add boiling water to fill mug an inch from the top. Drop the pat of butter into the mug (if using). Squeeze the lemon juice into the mug, then drop in the wedge. Serve with a spoon. ◇

CAPPUCCINO WITH MAPLE SHOT

My husband, Bruce, the barista in our house, once asked me if maple syrup would be good in cappuccino. I thought it sounded kind of strange and advised against it, but one night he prepared our cappuccino with pure maple syrup instead of the shot of vanilla-flavored syrup he usually uses. He hadn't told me about the substitution and watched me as I had my first sip. The cappuccino didn't shout "maple!" to me, but I noticed that it tasted particularly rich and deep, with toasty caramel notes; it was also less sweet than the version prepared with vanilla syrup, which sometimes gets cloying. If you have an espresso machine, give this a try. You might find, as I did, that it's a new favorite. **PER SERVING**

1 tablespoon maple syrup, plus additional for drizzling

cold, fresh milk—skim, low-fat, or whole
   (¾–1 cup, depending on mug size)

finely ground espresso

chocolate sundae syrup, optional but very good

Prepare the espresso machine so it is up to temperature and ready to steam. Pour 1 tablespoon maple syrup into a large mug; set aside. Add the milk to a metal pitcher (you can prepare two servings at once in a typical pitcher) and clip an espresso thermometer inside the pitcher so its tip is just below the milk's surface. Froth the milk with the steam wand, holding the pitcher at an angle with the tip of the steam wand just below the milk's surface; the milk should reach 150 degrees and should have a very creamy, frothy head. Set the pitcher aside; the milk temperature will rise another 5 degrees while it sits.

Pack a full measure of finely ground espresso into the filter basket and tamp it firmly. Pull a shot into a small pitcher or shot glass, then pour it into the mug; for a double (recommended), pull a second shot and add it to the mug. Immediately pour the steamed milk into the mug, holding back the froth with a spoon; fill the mug half to two-thirds full of steamed milk. Spoon the froth over the coffee, filling the mug to the brim. Drizzle a little maple syrup and a little chocolate syrup (if using) over the foam; serve immediately. ◇

MAPLE MALT

The traditional soda-fountain treat is the perfect vehicle for pure maple syrup. If you like, you can garnish the malt with a shot of whipped cream and a cherry; I prefer mine unadorned. **SERVES 2**

- 4 heaping scoops vanilla ice cream
- 1¼ cups whole or 2 percent milk, very cold
- ¼ cup maple syrup
- ¼ cup malted milk powder
- 4 shortbread cookies or vanilla wafers, optional

Combine all ingredients except cookies or wafers in blender. Cover tightly and pulse several times until ingredients are beginning to mix and the base of the blender is filled with liquid. Blend at regular speed for 30 to 45 seconds or until the consistency is the way you like it. Divide between two chilled malt glasses; garnish each with 2 cookies. Serve immediately. ◇

desserts

aple really shines in dessert recipes, where its sweet, rich flavor is allowed to come to the foreground rather than act as an accent. Homemade ice cream, rich pecan pie, and homey donut holes all rise to the next level when made with maple syrup. From kid-friendly maple crispy bars to sophisticated mini cream puffs with silky maple filling, there's something here for every palate.

Apple-Pear Pandowdy with Cranberries

Pandowdy is an old-fashioned pie with a top crust only; the recipe dates back to Colonial days. During baking, the crust is broken up and pushed slightly into the juices; it is this "dowdy" appearance that gives the dessert its name. **SERVES 6**

  1 tablespoon unsalted butter, plus additional for greasing casserole dish

1½ pounds Granny Smith, Braeburn, or other apples suitable for pie (about 3 large)

1½ pounds ripe pears (about 3 large or 4 medium)

  ½ cup whole fresh or frozen cranberries (thawed if frozen)

  2 tablespoons instant tapioca

  1 tablespoon freshly squeezed lemon juice

  ¼ teaspoon salt

  1 teaspoon whole Szechuan peppercorns, optional

  ⅔ cup maple syrup

    prepared pastry for single-crust pie

  1 tablespoon cream, half-and-half, or milk

1–2 tablespoons coarse sugar

>>

Heat oven to 400 degrees. Generously grease a round 2-quart casserole dish with butter; set aside. Peel, quarter, and core apples and pears; cut crosswise into ¼-inch-thick slices. In large mixing bowl, combine sliced apples and pears with cranberries, tapioca, lemon juice, and salt; stir gently and set aside.

Grind Szechuan peppercorns (if using) with mortar and pestle until evenly fine. Combine with syrup in small saucepan; if not using peppercorns, proceed as directed with just the syrup. Heat over medium-high heat until syrup boils, then reduce heat and cook for 5 minutes; watch carefully so syrup does not boil over (if it rises and threatens to boil over, immediately remove from heat, reduce heat, and return pan to heat). When syrup has cooked for 5 minutes, remove from heat and cool slightly, then pour into fruit mixture and stir gently to combine.

Transfer fruit mixture to prepared casserole dish. Dot with the 1 table-spoon butter, cut into small pieces. Place pastry on top, tucking edges under into the casserole to create a doubled edge (it will be lumpy and uneven; that's okay). Brush with cream; sprinkle with sugar. Bake for 20 minutes. Remove from oven; reduce heat to 350 degrees. Cut the crust into 2-inch squares; some of the edges will sink into the filling, and the top will be uneven. Return to oven and bake for 25 minutes or until the filling is bubbly and the top is browned and crisp. Cool for at least 25 minutes before serving; best served warm. ◇

MAPLE CRISPY BARS

When I decided to try using maple syrup in the traditional rice crispy bar recipe, I looked online for ideas, figuring there would be all kinds of maple versions out there. Surprisingly, there weren't. The few I found also included chocolate chips, white chocolate, brown sugar, and other add-ins, which I didn't want to try. So I simply cooked the maple syrup and butter together to caramelize it a bit before adding the marshmallows. The mellow caramel flavor is a nice addition to the traditional treats. **MAKES 18 BARS**

6 cups crisp rice cereal

⅓ cup maple syrup

4 tablespoons (½ stick) salted butter

4 cups mini marshmallows

Coat the inside of a very large mixing bowl and a 13x9–inch baking dish with cooking spray. Add the rice cereal to the mixing bowl. In a heavy-bottomed medium saucepan, combine syrup and butter. Cook over medium heat, stirring constantly with a wooden spoon, until butter melts and mixture turns bubbly. Continue to cook for 2 minutes longer, stirring constantly. Reduce heat to low and stir for about 30 seconds longer, then add the marshmallows and cook, stirring constantly, until the marshmallows melt and the mixture is smooth. Immediately scrape into the mixing bowl with the cereal and stir to mix thoroughly.

Transfer mixture to the prepared baking dish and spread out as best you can, then use a sheet of waxed paper to press the mixture evenly and firmly into the pan (or coat your hands with cooking spray and use them instead of the waxed paper). Cool for 5 minutes, then cut into 18 pieces—3 the long way and 6 across. Let cool completely in baking dish before transferring individual pieces to a serving plate. These bars are best the day they are made but can be stored in an airtight container for a day or two; they can also be frozen in an airtight container with waxed paper between the layers. ◇

MAPLE ICE CREAM

This traditional, rich ice cream, made with a cooked, egg-based custard which is then churned in an ice cream freezer, has a wonderful maple flavor. When you're preparing the custard mixture, be careful not to overcook it or it will curdle. Note: If you can find old-fashioned heavy cream which has not been ultra-pasteurized, your ice cream will have a fresher flavor, although the ultra-pasteurized cream will work. **MAKES ABOUT 1¼ QUARTS**

- 3 egg yolks
- 1 whole egg
- ¾ cup maple syrup
- 1½ cups heavy cream (see head note)
- 1 cup whole milk
- ½ teaspoon vanilla extract

Before you start, make sure your ice cream freezer will be ready when you need it; many require that you freeze the canister for 24 hours. You'll also need to prepare the cooked custard at least 6 hours in advance, to give it time to chill thoroughly.

When you're ready to prepare the ice cream custard, place egg yolks in medium mixing bowl and whisk until light in color and thickened slightly, about 2 minutes. Add whole egg and syrup and whisk until smooth; set aside. Place a wire-mesh strainer over a large, heat-proof mixing bowl and set aside.

In a heavy-bottomed medium saucepan, combine cream and milk. If you have a clip-on candy thermometer, position it in the saucepan, ensuring that the tip does not touch the bottom of the pan; alternatively, you can use a quick-read thermometer to check the progress of the custard during cooking. Heat the cream mixture over medium heat until bubbles appear around the edges. Pour about a cup of the hot cream mixture into the egg mixture, whisking the egg mixture constantly as you add the cream mixture; whisk until smooth. Pour the egg mixture into the saucepan with the remaining cream mixture and whisk until smooth. Cook over medium-low heat, stirring constantly, until the mixture thickens slightly and reaches 175 degrees; this will probably take 4 to 6 minutes. Remove saucepan from heat immediately and pour the mixture through the wire-mesh strainer into the clean mixing bowl. Stir vanilla into strained mixture. Let cool for about 20 minutes, then cover with a piece of plastic wrap, pressing it directly against the surface of the mixture. Cover the bowl with foil and chill for at least 6 hours or as long as overnight.

Churn the mixture in the prepared ice cream freezer according to the manufacturer's directions (in my countertop electric model, it takes about 25 minutes). Scrape ice cream into an airtight container and place in your freezer; it will become firmer after a few hours in the freezer. If it has become too firm when you want to serve it, let it stand at room temperature for 10 minutes before serving.

Variation: Maple-Nut Ice Cream

Toast ½ cup chopped pecans or walnuts in a dry cast-iron skillet over medium heat for about 5 minutes, stirring constantly. Transfer to a small bowl and set aside to cool completely (you can pop the bowl into the freezer for a few minutes to be sure that the nuts are not even the slightest bit warm when you use them). Add to the ice cream freezer during the last few minutes of freezing. ◇

PROFITEROLES (MINI CREAM PUFFS) WITH MAPLE CREAM

Although they look fancy, these miniature cream puffs with creamy maple filling are surprisingly easy to make. They are composed of two classic French ingredients, pâte à choux *(cream-puff pastry) and* crème anglaise *(English cream; also called pastry cream) which is enriched with maple in this version. Note: You may prepare the maple cream up to three days in advance and keep refrigerated until you're ready to use it, or you can prepare it just before making the puffs.* **MAKES ABOUT 30 PUFFS**

>>

MAPLE CREAM

⅔ cup maple syrup

1 cup whole milk, divided

½ teaspoon vanilla extract

3 egg yolks (save the whites for brushing the puffs, below)

2 tablespoons all-purpose flour

2 tablespoons cornstarch

MINI PUFFS

1 cup all-purpose flour

¼ teaspoon salt

1 cup whole milk

½ cup (1 stick) unsalted butter

4 eggs

....

Prepare the maple cream (see head note): In a heavy-bottomed small saucepan, heat syrup over medium heat without stirring until the surface is covered with foaming bubbles. Adjust heat so syrup boils vigorously but does not boil over and cook without stirring for 5 minutes. Remove from heat and stir in ½ cup milk and the vanilla; set aside. In a heavy-bottomed medium saucepan, whisk egg yolks and remaining ½ cup milk until well blended. Hold a small wire-mesh strainer over the saucepan containing the egg mixture and add the flour and cornstarch; shake to sift into egg yolks, then whisk until smooth. Whisking constantly, add warm syrup mixture to egg mixture in a thin stream; whisk until well blended. Cook over medium heat, whisking constantly (be sure to work the whisk into the corners of the saucepan to prevent the egg mixture from setting up), until mixture thickens; this will take about 3 minutes. Immediately scrape into a clean bowl and cool for 10 minutes, then press a piece of plastic wrap over the surface and cool to room temperature. If preparing more than an hour in advance, cover the bowl tightly with foil and refrigerate until needed.

Prepare the mini puffs: Heat oven to 400 degrees. Line two large baking sheets with parchment paper; set aside. In small bowl, stir together flour and salt. In a heavy-bottomed medium saucepan, heat milk and butter over medium heat, stirring occasionally, until butter melts and small bubbles form around the edges of the pan. Dump in the flour mixture all at once and beat vigorously with a wooden spoon until all flour has been incorporated and the dough looks fairly smooth. Reduce heat to low and cook, stirring constantly, for about 2 minutes; the dough should form a somewhat loose ball that pulls away from the sides of the pan. Drop the dough into a food processor and pulse a few times. Add the eggs one at a time, pulsing between each addition. When all eggs have been added, process for a minute longer; the dough should be smooth and shiny.

Spoon the dough into a pastry bag fitted with a star tip, and pipe it onto the baking sheets in mounds just a bit smaller than a golf ball, keeping them about an inch apart (alternatively, use two spoons to form the mounds). Beat reserved egg whites (from the maple cream) with a fork in a small bowl, then use a soft pastry brush to dab the egg whites over the tops of the puffs, using the brush to flatten the sharp point on top of each puff (if made with a pastry bag). Bake for 10 minutes, then reduce heat to 350 degrees and bake for 8 minutes longer. Next, switch positions of the two pans, also rotating them from front to back. Bake for 12 minutes longer; puffs should be nicely golden brown, and if you pick up a puff and tap the bottom with your finger, it should sound hollow. Remove baking sheets from oven and use a paring knife to make a small slit in the side of each puff, returning puffs to baking sheets as you go. Return to oven and bake for 5 minutes longer. Transfer puffs to a wire rack and set aside until completely cool.

To assemble the profiteroles, use a serrated knife to cut the side of each puff almost in half, leaving one side still connected like a hinge. Spoon about 2 teaspoons of the maple cream into each puff, pushing the top half slightly down over the cream. These are best when served promptly, although they can be refrigerated for up to an hour before serving. ◇

Maple Baklava

Browning the butter adds a nutty flavor that helps cut through the sweetness. Fair warning: preparing the baklava takes a good bit of time—at least two hours—so don't try to make this when you're in a hurry. Note: Before beginning, please read "Reducing Maple Syrup" on page 14 and "Testing a Thermometer" on page 16. Also note that two versions of the syrup are given below. They are both cooked and used in the same way, but one produces a moist, sticky baklava that is laden with syrup while the other has less syrup and produces a baklava that is less moist and more flaky. **MAKES 20 LARGE PIECES, PLUS A FEW SMALLER ODD-SHAPED PIECES**

....

½ pound chopped walnuts (about 2 cups)

½ pound slivered, blanched almonds (about 2 cups)

2 tablespoons sugar

1 teaspoon cinnamon

1¼ cups (2½ sticks) unsalted butter, cut into 1-inch chunks

1 pound phyllo sheets, thawed

SYRUP (TWO VERSIONS; SEE HEAD NOTE)

Ingredient	Moist, sticky baklava	Less moist, flaky baklava
maple syrup	2¼ cups	1¾ cups
water	¼ cup	¾ cup
sugar	¼ cup	¼ cup
lemon juice	2 tablespoons	1½ tablespoons
ground cardamom	½ teaspoon	½ teaspoon

....

Combine walnuts, almonds, sugar, and cinnamon in food processor. Pulse in very short bursts until the nuts are finely chopped; the texture should resemble very coarse sand with a few barley-size pieces. Set aside.

Begin heating oven to 350 degrees. Place butter in a heavy-bottomed stainless steel saucepan and melt over medium heat; the butter will be foamy (a stainless steel saucepan is important for browning the butter; if you use dark cookware, you won't be able to see how brown the butter is getting). Continue cooking, swirling pan occasionally, until the butter is sizzling and bubbling; the foam will dissipate and tiny brown flecks will form in the bottom of the saucepan. Remove from heat as soon as you see the flecks forming, then immediately pour the butter into a clean, cool saucepan or a metal bowl; this step prevents the butter from burning in the residual heat of the saucepan. Brush the insides of a 13x9–inch baking dish with some of the butter, then spoon off about ¼ cup of the butter from the top of the saucepan and transfer to a smaller bowl; set the smaller bowl aside.

Unroll the phyllo on your work surface. If it is larger than your baking dish, use a sharp chef's knife to trim it so it is about the same size as the top of the dish; discard the trimmings. Cover the phyllo with a barely damp towel (I spray the towel with a mister, which is the perfect amount of water); you will have to lift the towel each time you get a sheet of phyllo, which may seem like a hassle, but if you don't keep the stack covered the phyllo will dry out and be hard to work with.

Lay one sheet of phyllo in the prepared dish, keeping it as intact as possible. Brush the sheet *lightly* with the melted butter from the saucepan using a soft pastry brush. Repeat with 9 more sheets of phyllo (for a total of 10 sheets), brushing each with butter. Spread a third of the nut mixture (a little more than 1⅓ cups) evenly over the phyllo. Lay 8 more sheets of phyllo in the dish, again brushing each with butter (the first sheet on top of the nuts will slip around, but you can gently hold the center down with your free hand and dab/brush outward toward the edges). Spread half of the remaining nut mixture evenly over top. Lay 8 more sheets of phyllo in the dish, brushing each with butter. Spread remaining nut mixture evenly over top, then lay 10 more sheets of phyllo in the dish, brushing

>>

each with butter; for the last few sheets, use the butter you spooned into the small bowl (which won't be as browned as any butter remaining in the saucepan). You'll probably have some butter left; transfer it to a small container and seal tightly, then refrigerate and use for other cooking.

Use a very sharp knife to cut the assembled pastry lengthwise into 4 equal strips, cutting just through the top layer (10 sheets) of phyllo; you'll feel the knife break through the phyllo and hit the nut layer. Now start at one corner and make 5 shallow cuts at an angle across the first cuts, again cutting just through the top layer; when you're done you'll have cut the top layer of pastry into 20 evenly sized diamonds and a few odd-shaped corners. One corner will need a short additional angled cut because it will be irregularly shaped and larger than the other pieces. Use a spray mister to mist the top very lightly with cool water; if you don't have a mister, use your fingertips to sprinkle a few drops of water over the top. Bake for 40 minutes or until the phyllo is nicely browned on the top, sides, and bottom (meanwhile, you'll be preparing the syrup; see next step below). Remove from oven and set on a heatproof surface.

As soon as the baklava is in the oven, make the syrup: In a heavy-bottomed 1-gallon soup pot or other deep, heavy saucepan, combine syrup, water, sugar, lemon juice, and cardamom. Clip a tested candy thermometer (see head note) to the side of the pan, ensuring that the tip does not touch the bottom of the pan. Cook over medium-high heat, stirring constantly with a wooden spoon until sugar has dissolved. Continue cooking without stirring until the surface is covered with foaming bubbles, then adjust heat so mixture continues to bubble but does not boil over and cook without stirring until mixture reaches 13 degrees above boiling (225 degrees if your thermometer measures boiling water at 212 degrees); this will probably take 8 to 12 minutes from the time the mixture starts boiling for the moist, sticky baklava or 15 to 20 minutes for the less moist, flaky baklava. Remove from heat and set aside.

When the baklava is out of the oven, let it stand for about 15 minutes, then use a ladle to drizzle about a third of the warm syrup evenly over the cuts. Let stand for 10 minutes, then cut all the way through all layers, following the lines you cut before baking. Pour remaining syrup over the top, ensuring that each cut line gets some of the syrup. Let the baklava stand for at least 4 hours to absorb the syrup before serving; if you don't want to serve the baklava yet, cover the pan with foil. The baklava actually is better the next day, and it can be stored at room temperature, covered with foil, for up to 5 days. To serve, pry out one of the odd-shaped corner pieces with a fork, then use a fork to lift out the full-size pieces. You may want to cut the full-size pieces in half, as the baklava is very rich. ◊

SHORTBREAD WITH MAPLE CARAMEL AND SEA SALT

Sea salt is often used to garnish sweets. In these rich bar cookies, its delicate texture provides a subtle but wonderful crunch and the tang of the salt is a pleasant contrast to the buttery, maple-rich caramel. Maple caramel is a bit fussy and time-consuming to make, but the results are worth it; take your time and don't try to rush it. Note: Before beginning, please read "Reducing Maple Syrup" on page 14 and "Testing a Thermometer" on page 16. Also, note that you should not raise the heat above medium while you are cooking the syrup mixture for the caramel. **MAKES 36 BARS**

¾ cup (1½ sticks) unsalted butter, softened

¼ cup sugar

1 egg yolk

1 teaspoon vanilla extract

1½ cups all-purpose flour

CARAMEL TOPPING

⅔ cup heavy cream

3 tablespoons unsalted butter

1 cup maple syrup

2 tablespoons corn syrup

½ teaspoon vanilla extract

sea salt flakes (large, soft flakes such as Maldon work best here)

>>

Heat oven to 350 degrees for a glass dish or to 375 degrees for a metal pan. Coat a 9x9–inch baking dish lightly with cooking spray. Cut a 15x9–inch piece of parchment paper, then line the bottom and two sides of the dish with it, smoothing it firmly into place in the bottom and up the sides and allowing it to hang over the edges. Spray parchment lightly with cooking spray and set dish aside.

In mixing bowl, beat butter and sugar with an electric mixer on high speed until light and fluffy. Beat in egg yolk and vanilla. Add flour and beat on low speed until well combined. Transfer to prepared baking dish and use a rubber spatula to smooth evenly into the bottom. Bake for 20 to 25 minutes or until the center is lightly golden and the edges are just barely starting to brown and have begun to pull away from the pan slightly; don't overcook or it will fall apart when cut. Set aside on a wire rack while you prepare the caramel topping.

To prepare the topping, combine cream and butter in microwave-safe 2-cup measure or medium mixing bowl. Microwave at 70 percent power, stirring after about a minute, until butter has melted and mixture begins to bubble and foam up, 1½ to 2 minutes total. Set aside at room temperature.

In heavy-bottomed medium saucepan, heat maple syrup and corn syrup over medium heat, stirring until mixture is well blended, then continue to cook without stirring until the surface is covered with foaming bubbles. Reduce heat slightly so mixture boils but does not boil over and cook without stirring, swirling pan occasionally to keep the bubbling down and adjusting the heat as needed, until mixture reaches 35 degrees above boiling on a tested quick-read thermometer (see head note; 247 degrees if your thermometer measures boiling water at 212 degrees); this will probably take 15 to 25 minutes from the time the mixture starts boiling. Remove from heat and let stand for 3 minutes.

Add cream mixture in a thin stream to the mixture in the saucepan, stirring constantly, and return to medium-low heat. Cook, stirring frequently for the first 5 minutes, until mixture returns to 35 degrees above boiling; this will probably take 15 to 20 minutes. Remove from heat and stir in vanilla. Immediately pour over shortbread without scraping out the bottom of the saucepan (you can scrape the side of the pan where the caramel is pouring). Quickly tilt the pan of shortbread slightly so the topping flows to all corners and edges. (Once the saucepan cools a bit, you can use a spoon to dig out the hardening caramel and enjoy it as a cook's bonus.) Let stand at room temperature until topping is completely cool, about an hour, then cover pan and refrigerate for at least 2 hours.

Use a thin metal spatula coated with cooking spray to loosen the caramel from the two edges that don't have parchment; you may have to rock the spatula blade to get it to slip between the pan and the caramel. Use the parchment to lift the shortbread out in one piece, transferring it to a cutting board. With a very sharp chef's knife or other long knife, cut into 6 strips of equal width, using a slight sawing motion with the knife (if you push straight down, the pressure needed to cut the caramel might crumble the shortbread; if you're really having problems with crumbling you can flip the shortbread over, caramel-side down, so the knife cuts through the crumbly shortbread before encountering the caramel). Working with one strip at a time, cut each strip into 6 squares. Sprinkle lightly with sea salt, pressing it in gently. These bars are best served at room temperature or slightly cool but should be stored in the refrigerator because the caramel may soften and run slightly after a while at room temperature. ◇

APPLE DONUT HOLES WITH MAPLE GLAZE

These tasty little treats are actually somewhere between a donut hole and a fritter. Dried apples that have been rehydrated in maple syrup provide a wonderful, chewy texture and rich maple flavor; the glaze adds an extra hit of maple and an attractive finish. Note: The syrup in the batter causes these to get very deep brown when they're fried, so you need to make the balls small enough that the donut holes cook inside before burning outside.

MAKES ABOUT 30 DONUT HOLES

>>

½ cup chopped dried apple slices (chopped medium to medium fine before measuring; about 1¼ ounces)

⅔ cup maple syrup

1 tablespoon unsalted butter

1–1½ quarts vegetable oil for deep frying

POWDERED SUGAR GLAZE

1½ cups powdered sugar

¼ cup maple syrup

¼ cup whole or 2 percent milk

DOUGH

2 cups all-purpose flour

1½ teaspoons baking powder

½ teaspoon salt

¼ teaspoon cinnamon

¼ teaspoon baking soda

1 egg

⅓ cup heavy cream or half-and-half, plus a little more if needed

In a heavy-bottomed small saucepan, combine apples, syrup, and butter. Heat just to boiling, stirring several times. Reduce heat and simmer for 8 minutes, stirring occasionally; the syrup should be somewhat thickened so the liquid is saucelike. Remove from heat and set aside until completely cool.

When you're ready to mix and cook the donut holes, begin heating about 2½ inches of oil in a deep fryer or heavy pot that has a deep-frying thermometer clipped to the side; the oil needs to be 375 degrees when you start frying. While the oil is heating, line a large baking sheet with newspaper, then cover with several layers of paper towels; you'll also need a wire cooling rack and long sheet of waxed paper. Combine all glaze ingredients in a small bowl, stirring until smooth. Now set up your work area; you'll be removing the donut holes from the oil and placing them on the paper towels to drain, then rolling them in the glaze, then transferring them to the wire rack, so you'll want to arrange everything in a logical fashion, close together to catch drips.

Sift together flour, baking powder, salt, cinnamon, and baking soda in a large mixing bowl. In a small bowl, beat together the egg and ⅓ cup of the cream with a fork until smooth. Add egg mixture to apple mixture and stir until very well combined, then scrape into flour mixture and stir with a wooden spoon until as well mixed as possible. Add additional cream as needed, stirring until all flour has been incorporated and the dough is firm enough to shape with your hands (rather like the type of cookie dough you'd form into balls before baking, perhaps just a little firmer); the dough should not be wet or runny.

Pinch off enough dough to make a ball about an inch across, rolling it fairly firmly between your palms. Use a slotted spoon to slide the ball into the 375-degree oil. Cook until the surface is deeply browned, 2½ to 3 minutes, rotating the ball almost constantly with the slotted spoon. Remove the donut hole with the slotted spoon, allowing it to drain briefly over the pot before transferring it to the paper towels. Let cool for a minute or so, then cut it in half to check doneness; if it's underdone, make the next balls a bit smaller or cook just a bit longer. Shape 3 more dough balls and cook until deeply browned and cooked through. Transfer to the paper towels and let cool for about 30 seconds, then roll one in the bowl of glaze; use a fork to transfer the glazed donut hole to the wire rack, then glaze the other 2 donut holes. Continue shaping, cooking, and glazing remaining dough, 3 balls at a time; adjust heat as necessary to maintain the oil temperature as close to 375 degrees as possible.

Variation: Syrup-Glazed Donut Holes

Omit the powdered sugar glaze. Warm about ¾ cup maple syrup in a microwave-safe medium mixing bowl. Roll the hot donut holes in the warm maple syrup as directed for the powdered sugar glaze, transferring to the wire rack with a fork. ◇

MAPLE-PECAN PIE

A classic pecan pie jazzed up with maple syrup. The toasted pecans are a great complement to the maple and help balance the sweetness, although you can skip the toasting step if you prefer. It's important to use a deep-dish pie plate as specified; the filling would probably overflow a standard-size crust. The whipped cream helps cut the sweetness, especially if you add only a touch of sugar to the cream as you're whipping it (you are making homemade whipped cream for this, aren't you?!). **MAKES 1 PIE**

1¾ cups coarsely chopped pecans (about 6 ounces)

prepared pastry for single-crust pie

1 cup maple syrup (for a richer flavor, use half grade B and half grade A)

¾ cup packed light brown sugar

3 tablespoons unsalted butter, melted

1 tablespoon all-purpose flour

1 tablespoon bourbon or dark rum, optional

½ teaspoon salt

3 eggs

1 teaspoon vanilla extract

whipped cream for serving, optional

Heat oven to 375 degrees. Place pecans on a rimmed baking sheet and toast for 5 minutes or until lightly browned, stirring several times. Transfer nuts to a bowl to cool for about 10 minutes; rinse and dry baking sheet. Reduce oven to 350 degrees.

Line deep-dish pie plate with pastry; decoratively flute edges and place on cleaned baking sheet (to catch drips). Combine syrup, brown sugar, butter, flour, bourbon (if using), and salt in medium mixing bowl; whisk until well blended. Add eggs and vanilla, and whisk until smooth. Scatter pecans evenly in crust; pour filling over nuts. Bake until filling is golden brown and set, 45 to 60 minutes; cover crust loosely with strips of foil during the last 15 to 20 minutes of baking if it is over-browning. Place pie on wire rack and let cool completely before serving, with whipped cream if you like. ◊

INDIVIDUAL APPLE PASTRIES

These are lovely to look at and even better to eat. Try to keep the gooey caramel sauce from dripping over the edges of the puff pastry when you're arranging the apples on top; otherwise, the sauce "glues" down the edges of the pastry so it doesn't puff up properly. You'll have a bit of caramel left in the skillet after you assemble the pastries—pan-scraping, spoon-licking heaven, but be sure to let it cool for fifteen minutes or so before indulging. The caramel is shockingly hot and sticky, and it could seriously burn your tongue, fingers, or anything else it touches until it has cooled down. Note: Be sure to use medium-size apples rather than large ones: the apple wedges have to be narrower than the pastry squares. **MAKES 9 PASTRIES**

....

1 sheet puff pastry (half of a 17.3-ounce package), thawed

2 medium apples suitable for pie, such as Jazz, Honeycrisp, or Braeburn (see head note)

½ teaspoon ground ginger

½ cup maple syrup

1½ tablespoons unsalted butter, divided

¼ cup sliced almonds

....

Heat oven to 375 degrees. Line a 10x15–inch jelly roll pan (or two smaller baking sheets) with parchment paper. Unfold puff pastry sheet on lightly floured work surface. Roll the pastry to a 10½-inch square. Cut into 9

>>

pieces, each 3½ inches square. Arrange about ¼ inch apart on prepared baking sheet. Prick each square several times with a fork. Refrigerate pastry while you prepare the apples.

Quarter each unpeeled apple and cut away the core; cut the quarters so that two quarters from each apple come out slightly thicker than the other two because you'll be cutting the quarters into thinner wedges, and you need 18 of them from each apple. Pick out the two largest quarters from each apple and cut each into 5 wedges; cut the remaining quarters into 4 wedges each.

Add ginger to syrup in measuring cup and blend well with a fork. Pour half of the syrup mixture into a large, heavy-bottomed skillet, then add half of the butter. Cook over medium heat until butter melts, stirring several times. Add half of the apple slices in a single layer. Cook for 5 minutes, swirling pan frequently to prevent sticking and using a fork like a spatula to carefully turn each slice halfway through; don't poke the apples with the fork, simply slip it underneath each slice. The syrup should be quite bubbly and reduced, but if it is reducing too quickly and threatening to burn, remove the skillet from the heat and reduce the temperature before continuing. After 5 minutes, remove the skillet from the heat.

Use the fork to lift up an apple slice (again, don't poke the apple), using a second fork to coax it onto the first fork if necessary. Place the apple slice on one of the pastry squares with the curved edge close to one side; be careful not to drip the reduced maple caramel over the edges of the pastry square (see head note). Continue to transfer apples, neatly arranging 4 slices on each square in an overlapping layer; repeat until you've topped half of the squares. Repeat cooking and topping with remaining syrup mixture, butter, and apples. Scatter almonds evenly over the apples. Bake until pastry is puffed and golden, 15 to 20 minutes. Transfer pastries immediately to a wire rack. Cool for at least 15 minutes before serving; may be served warm or at room temperature. ◇

WARTIME NUT WAFERS

This basic recipe is adapted from Sweets Without Sugar, *a book written by Marion White during World War II. Along with many other foods, sugar was rationed during the war, and home cooks often had to bake with substitutes such as molasses, corn syrup, honey—and maple syrup. Of the several recipes I tried from this book, I particularly enjoyed these easy refrigerator cookies; their texture is somewhat like shortbread.* **MAKES ABOUT 24 COOKIES**

....

½ cup (1 stick) unsalted butter, softened

1 cup maple syrup

1 egg yolk

2 cups all-purpose flour, plus additional as needed

1 teaspoon baking powder

¼ teaspoon salt

1 cup chopped pecans or other nuts (about 4 ounces)

....

In large mixing bowl, beat butter with electric mixer until fluffy. Add syrup and egg yolk and beat until very well combined, scraping down bowl as needed. Sift flour, baking powder, and salt together into a medium mixing bowl. Add about half of the flour mixture to the syrup mixture and beat with the mixer until smooth. Add remaining flour and stir in with a rubber spatula. Stir in nuts. If mixture seems too soft and sticky to shape, stir in a little more flour, a tablespoon at a time.

Tear off a 20-inch length of waxed paper and place it on your work surface, then scrape the dough in a thick line fairly close to one long edge; use the rubber spatula to shape the dough into a rough log about 12 inches long. Roll up the waxed paper tightly, then twist the ends to help maintain the shape. Place on a baking sheet for support and refrigerate for an hour. Turn the log over so the opposite side is down; this will give the cookies a rounded rectangle shape with two flat sides. Refrigerate overnight.

>>

When you're ready to bake, heat oven to 450 degrees. Coat a large baking sheet with cooking spray. Use a very sharp knife to slice the log into ¼-inch-thick rounds, placing on prepared baking sheet about ½ inch apart. Bake for 10 minutes or until lightly browned.

Sweets Without Sugar is in the public domain and has been digitized by Google; you can see the entire book by searching the catalog at hathitrust.org.

◊

Backyard sugaring:
making maple
syrup *in* your yard

It's surprisingly easy to tap the maple trees in your yard—and you may be amazed by how much finished syrup you can get, even if you have a city lot with only one or two maples. Any *healthy* maple tree that's big enough (see below) can be tapped. Sugar content of the sap varies among maple species; sugar maples typically produce the sweetest sap, while boxelders—actually a type of maple—produce sap with the lowest sugar concentrations (see page 2 for more information on maple species used for tapping).

Before tapping, make sure the tree is large enough that you can drill a taphole without injuring the tree. Minimum tree diameter is 10 inches, which is a little over 31 inches around. A maple tree this size can support one tap; if the tree has a 14-inch diameter (44 inches around), you could put a second tap in the tree if it is completely healthy. (If the tree is unhealthy or shows any signs of disease or stress, don't tap it at all.)

EQUIPMENT NEEDED

For each taphole, you'll need a collection system that starts with a tube, called a *spile,* that gets inserted into a hole you'll drill in the tree. Use half-inch copper or PVC pipe, available in the plumbing department at home centers, to make spiles; if you're using PVC, buy the white kind that's used for water supply, not the black stuff used for waste pipes. Cut the pipe into three- or four-inch pieces with a hacksaw and file the edges smooth; if you're using copper, a tubing cutter works great and your spiles won't need filing.

Each taphole will need at least one collection vessel. Plastic gallon jugs that held water or milk can be hung on the tree and work great at the start of the season when the sap is just starting to flow. Use a razor knife to carefully cut a hole for the spile in the top part of the jug, near the handle (visible in the photo on page 154). The tighter the spile fits the better, preventing rain, bark, and dirt from getting into the sap.

You'll also need a piece of stiff, heavy wire (such as stovepipe wire or a coat hanger) and a nail with a large head.

When the sap really starts running, switch to a five-gallon food-grade pail or a large water jug used for camping; these will sit on the ground. You'll need about five feet of food-grade flexible plastic tubing, available at home-brewing supply stores, to run between the spile and the pail; the tubing must fit snugly over the end of the spile, so take one along when you go shopping. Once you have the flexible tubing, cut a hole in the pail lid that's just large enough to squeeze the flexible tubing through; if you're using a camping jug, simply run the tubing into the spout opening.

Cooking sap in home-size batches is easiest in two stages. The first should be done outside, because of the tremendous amount of water vapor that is released. You don't want to boil off several gallons of sugary water on your kitchen stove; that amount of sticky steam isn't good for your walls, ceiling, or furniture.

For outdoor heat, a propane burner like those used to deep-fry turkeys works well, although you'll go through a lot of propane. A wood fire is more traditional and costs a lot less than propane; an outdoor fire pit that you can put a grate over to hold the pot is a perfect setup. For the pot, a three-gallon stockpot works fine, although larger is better. I prefer stainless steel or anodized aluminum, but I've also used a plain aluminum stockpot for the outdoor boil.

Once the sap has reduced as described later, you'll strain it into a smaller "finishing" pot for the final cooking. I use a wire-mesh strainer, lined with a square from a clean white cotton t-shirt. The finishing pot must have a heavy bottom to prevent scorching, and it needs to be large enough to prevent the sap from overflowing if it boils up. Here, I strongly prefer stainless steel to aluminum, which some feel may impart an off-flavor at this stage. My favorite finishing pot is a heavy-bottomed one-gallon soup pot that is about five inches deep.

Most home-based syrup makers use a candy thermometer to test the syrup for doneness. For the final cooking, you'll need basic kitchen equipment like potholders, tongs, and perhaps a funnel. You'll also need clean bottles or jars to store your finished syrup in. I use half-pint canning jars with new lids and process the jars in a hot-water canning bath at the end so I don't have to refrigerate the finished syrup.

TAPPING THE TREES: WHEN AND HOW

Set your taps out when the temperature starts to rise above freezing during the day but still drops below freezing at night. In our area, this usually happens at the beginning of March, but it can be as early as mid-February. Don't set your taps out too early: the holes may dry out if they are open too long before the sap starts flowing.

Before you head outside, wash your spiles and jugs (and flexible plastic tubing, if using) very thoroughly in hot water; most sugarers don't use soap on their equipment because it may leave a residue that could contaminate the syrup.

There are many opinions about the best location for the taphole. Many say that the south side of the tree is best. Others feel that the hole should be directly above a large root or below a main branch. In one piece I read, the author was convinced that the hole should be no higher than four or five inches from the ground, because that is where the flow is best. I've noticed that larger operations make tapholes at a height convenient for drilling and that they move around the tree from year to year, so that's what I do. The south side is a good place to start, but if you're putting two tapholes in the same tree, the second hole should be on a different side of the tree (and in subsequent years, you need to stay at least nine inches above or below the previous year's hole or at least four inches to one side).

Fit an electric or cordless drill with a ⅝-inch spade bit. Hold the bit against the tree at a slight upward angle, and drill 1½ to 2 inches deep—

no more (see photo at left). Use a coffee cup to toss some warm water into the hole to clear the sawdust. Place a spile into the hole, and tap in firmly with a mallet or hammer (see photo below); if using a metal hammer, put a small block of wood over the end of the spile to prevent crushing. Don't pound too hard, or you could split the wood; trees are brittle in cold weather. If the spile is loose, pull it out and wrap a strip of duct tape around it, then try again; if it's too tight, re-drill the hole, rotating the spade bit around slightly to enlarge the opening.

< Drilling a hole

If you're using a hanging jug, position the capped jug so the spile slips into the hole you cut near the top (see photo on next page). Make a double loop of the heavy wire around the jug's handle, then pound a nail in the tree above the jug so the loop fits snugly over the nail. This setup takes the weight of the sap off the spile so it doesn't get pulled out when the jug is full. If you're using a pail on the ground to collect sap, slip the flexible tubing over the spile, then work the other end into the hole you cut in the lid of the pail. The large

< Pounding a spile

Hanging a jug ›

spout opening on a camping jug should be covered up to prevent debris from getting in. Cut off the corner of a heavyweight plastic bag, then run the flexible tubing through that and into the jug; you need to have enough tubing in the jug to prevent it from slipping back out. Once the tubing is positioned, push the plastic bag down to cover the spout opening, then use freezer tape, wrapped tightly around the cut corner of the bag, to secure the bag around the tubing.

FROM SAP TO SYRUP

You'll need at least five gallons of sap before boiling or you won't have enough, by the time it reduces, for the final cooking; there will be so little in the pan that it will just burn. If the sap flow is slow, freeze small amounts each day until you've accumulated enough; you can also store it outside in tightly capped jugs until you have enough, as long as the weather remains cold. Keep it in the shade (preferably in a snowbank), and don't store it longer than a few days without freezing or the sap could sour.

When you have enough sap, start cooking outside in your large stockpot. If the sap is flowing well, you can add more to the pot over the course of the day; keep approximate track of the amount you add so you know what yield to expect. (Plan on about 1 pint of finished syrup per 5 gallons of sap as a rough rule of thumb.)

Once the sap has reduced to a few quarts—or whatever will fit into your finishing pot—get your finishing equipment ready. Boil your straining cloth in a pan of water for a few minutes; pull it out with tongs, and when it's cool enough to handle, wring it out and use it to line a wire-mesh strainer. Place this atop your finishing pot, and carefully pour the hot sap through the strainer. Most home syrup makers do the final cooking indoors, on the kitchen stove.

Cook the sap in the finishing pot over high heat until it starts boiling, then adjust the heat so the sap boils steadily and vigorously but does not boil over. By law, syrup sold commercially must have a sugar content of 66 percent. To reach this level, the sap needs to be reduced until it reaches 7 degrees above the boiling point of water. For the most consistent, accurate results, use a candy thermometer to judge doneness; please read "Reducing Maple Syrup" on page 14 and "Testing a Thermometer" on page 16 for tips that will help you get an accurate reading. Keep your eye on the thermometer throughout the final boil but especially once it starts getting near the 7-degrees-F-above-boiling mark; the temperature rises very quickly at the end and the sap can also boil over easily. You need to watch it constantly. Remove it from the heat the instant it reaches 7 degrees above boiling; if you overcook it, the syrup will begin crystallizing during storage.

You can also judge doneness without a thermometer by using the old-fashioned "apron test." Watch the patterns of bubbles on the surface of the boiling sap. When it is close to the proper stage, the liquid will start forming large bubbles, about an inch across, and there will be occasional "eruptions" of bubble clusters around the edges of the pot. Don't let your attention waver for an instant at this stage, because the syrup can easily boil over. When the surface is covered with small bubbles and is just beginning to foam, dip a cool metal spatula or large metal spoon into the syrup and hold it away from the pot, over a plate. The syrup will drip off quickly at first, but when the last drops run together and slide off in a small sheet (called an *apron*), the syrup is done

Sugar sand >

and should be removed from the heat immediately.

The finished syrup usually still contains minute particles, which eventually settle to the bottom of the jar as a cloudy, hazy layer. This residue is called *sugar sand,* and although it is edible, it looks unappealing. Commercial syrup processors use special felt filters to remove these particles before bottling; the heavy material soaks up a lot of syrup, though, so it isn't practical for small-batch processing because you'll lose too much of your precious syrup. Instead, pour the finished, still-hot syrup into a clean jar; let it cool, then store it in the fridge, tightly covered, for a week or so, until any sugar sand in the bottom has firmed up (see photo above). Carefully pour the clear syrup into clean jars for storage, stopping when you reach the cloudy layer; use the cloudy syrup for cooking. Store your syrup in the refrigerator, where it will keep for many months; you can also freeze it for extended storage.

You may also seal the finished syrup in a hot-water-bath canner; canned syrup may be stored in a cool location, unrefrigerated, for a year or more. Re-heat the clear syrup (after pouring it away from the sugar sand) until it is just beginning to boil, then pour into sterilized half-pint jars and process for ten minutes in boiling water, following the same procedures you would for homemade jam; the *Ball Blue Book* is the standard reference for canning instructions.

Home-processed syrup may be lighter in color than commercial syrup you're used to seeing, especially at the start of the season; as explained on page 3, there are four grades of commercially produced syrup, and the lightest grade is seldom seen in the store. As the season progresses, your finished syrup will appear darker. When the sap develops a brownish tinge and becomes cloudy, it's time to stop collecting it. At this point, the trees have started to bud, and syrup made from "buddy" sap has a harsh flavor. Wash your equipment in hot, clear water (without soap), and pack it away until next year.

If you're wondering what happens to your lovely maple trees once you've drilled holes in them, don't fret. By the end of the summer, the holes will be partially filled in with new wood. The next year, when you drill your tapholes, you'll be able to see the "belly buttons" from last year's tapholes (remember to drill new holes nine inches above or below last year's holes or four inches to the side around the tree). By fall the second year, bark has usually grown over the year-and-a-half-old hole, and by the following syrup season there may be just a faint scar to show the two-year-old hole. Nature heals, and tapped maples continue to provide sweet sap for our enjoyment for many years. ◊

notes

1. The scientific names for the various maples discussed are as follows: sugar maple, *Acer saccharum;* silver maple, *A. saccharinum;* red maple, *A. rubrum;* black maple, *A. nigrum;* boxelder, *A. negundo;* Norway maple, *A. platanoides.*

2. U.S. Department of Agriculture, Natural Resources Conservation Service, *The PLANTS Database* (Greensboro, NC: National Plant Data Team, 2012), available: http://plants.usda.gov.

   An extended freeze-thaw cycle is crucial to maple syrup production, no matter where the trees are growing. The winter of 2011–12 was exceptionally mild in the Upper Midwest; in Minneapolis, for example, temperatures were 70 degrees or above for eight days in March, and overnight lows were above freezing for much of the month. The sap flow was highly irregular, and once sap did start to flow it became buddy very quickly. As a result, most syrup producers in the Upper Midwest—hobbyists and commercial operators alike—produced very little if any maple syrup in the spring of 2012.

   Maple syrup production information from the U.S. Department of Agriculture and Statistics Canada: http://northamericanmaple.org/images/stories/CropReport/2011USMapleCrop.pdf and www.statcan.gc.ca/pub/23-221-x/2011000/part-partie1-eng.htm.

3. The seventeenth-century Franciscan missionary Chrestien Leclercq, who worked extensively with the Micmac Algonquin tribe in Canada, wrote that he ate and drank as the Indians did, noting that maple sap was "considered a precious remedy" for persons suffering from "indisposition."

Henri Joutel, a French soldier and historian who traveled in the 1680s with the LaSalle expedition to Texas, commented that when they arrived at Chicagou (Chicago), they "did not have much food, but Providence gave us, to mix with our cornmeal, a manna, the sap obtained from maples which are common and very large in this region." Presumably, expedition members secured this knowledge about local foods from the Ho-Chunk or the Illini Indians who were, at that time, the only permanent inhabitants of the area. V. Havard, "Drink Plants of the North American Indians," *Bulletin of the Torrey Botanical Club* 23.2 (Lancaster, PA: Torrey Botanical Society, February 29, 1896), 42, available: http://www.jstor.org/stable/2478422.

4. Havard, "Drink Plants," 42–43.

5. Frances Densmore, "Uses of Plants by the Chippewa Indians," *Forty-fourth Annual Report of the Bureau of American Ethnology to the Secretary of the Smithsonian Institution, 1926–1927* (Washington, DC: U.S. Government Printing Office, 1928), 308–13. Densmore's entire report was reprinted as *How Indians Use Wild Plants for Food, Medicine & Crafts* (New York: Dover Publications, Inc., 1974).

6. Some Indian tribes, such as members of the Iroquois Confederacy who lived around Onondaga Lake in New York, did use salt, which they extracted from saline springs on the lake's shore. Jesuit missionaries who visited the area in the mid-seventeenth century noted "a salt spring on the margin of the lake, situated very close to a fresh-water spring . . . The Indians had a rude process of manufacture before the English

occupied the region" ("Salt Springs of On-ondaga: History of the Development of a Great Industry," *New York Times,* January 16, 1894). Other Eastern Woodlands tribes were close to saline springs from which they extracted salt, particularly those near Equality and Shawneetown, Illinois, as well as some in southern Ohio [Ian W. Brown, *The Role of Salt in Eastern North American Prehistory* (Baton Rouge, LA: Department of Culture, Recreation and Tourism; Louisi-ana Archaeological Survey and Antiquities Commission, 1981)], available: http://www.crt.state.la.us/archaeology/virtualbooks/SALT/hist.htm).

Densmore, "Uses of Plants," 318. Note that once Indians learned to use salt, it rose in importance; indeed, the Treaty with the Pillager Band of Chippewa Indians (often referred to as the Salt Treaty), made in 1847 between the Pillager Band in Minnesota and the U.S. government, stipulated that the band should receive, among other goods, "thirty nests (fourteen each) heavy tin kettles, five hundred pounds of tobacco, and five barrels of salt" in exchange for the land "Beginning at the south end of Otter-Tail Lake: thence southerly on the boundary-line between the Sioux and Chip-peway Indians to Long Prairie River; thence up said river to Crow Wing River; thence up Crow Wing River to Leaf River; thence up Leaf River to the head of said river; and from thence in a direct line to the place of beginning" [Charles J. Kappler, ed., *Indian Affairs: Laws and Treaties; Vol. II, Treaties* (Washington, DC: Government Printing Office, 1904), 569–70]. It is interesting to note that heavy tin kettles were part of the settlement included in the treaty; one may assume that some of these, at least, found their way to the Indians' sugar camps.

7. Thomas Vennum, Jr., *Wild Rice and the Ojib-way People* (St. Paul: Minnesota Historical Society Press, 1988), 204–6.

8. Julian P. Boyd, Charles T. Cullen, John Catanzariti, and Barbara B. Oberg, et al, eds., *The Papers of Thomas Jefferson* (Princeton, NJ: Princeton University Press, 1950–), available: http://www.monticello.org/site/house-and-gardens.

9. *Walton's Vermont Register and Farmer's Almanac for 1840* (Montpelier, VT: E. P. Walton and Sons, 1840), available: http://ia600200.us.archive.org/14/items/vermontyrbook18401846ches/vermontyrbook18401846ches.pdf.

10. Marion White, *Sweets Without Sugar* (Garden City, NY: Blue Ribbon Books, 1945), 9, available: http://catalog.hathitrust.org/Record/010746425.

11. Dr. Trubek's work is ongoing as of this writing; for information on the fascinating studies she has done on maple syrup and other foods, check out her pioneering book, *The Taste of Place* (Berkeley and Los Angeles: University of California Press, 2009).

12. For further discussion, see "The Political Economy of Wild Rice Indigenous Heri-tage and University Research" by Winona LaDuke, available: multinationalmonitor.org/mm2004/042004/laduke.html.

INDEX